3 WORST MEDS

MEDS

YOU'RE PROBABLY TAKING

Chemist Shows How to
Ditch Risky Meds Before
They Sabotage Your Health

SHANE ELLISON, MS

Shane Ellison, MS
3 Worst Meds You're Probably Taking
ISBN: 978-0-692-96841-3

HEALTH MYTHS PUBLISHING
Support@HealthMyths.net

Printed in Canada

TABLE OF CONTENTS

3 Worst Meds
You're Probably Taking

by Heart Surgeon, Dr. Dwight Lundell, MD

For anyone who's been told that their life depends on meds,
3 Worst Meds is a must-read—a life preserver in a tumultuous sea
of lies and highly organized deceit

When Shane asked me to meet, I did a little background research on him first. I wondered what I—a mainstream heart surgeon—would possibly have to talk about with a "rogue chemist" who quit his great job at one of the most prestigious drug companies, Eli Lilly? Coincidentally, that's the same drug company that gave me my first "bribe." (Er, I mean, gift.) It was a black doctor's bag with my name embossed in gold letters on the front. It took me awhile to see how I was being enticed to push meds . . . I still have it today.

We met over lunch at Whole Foods. Like Shane, I too studied chemistry in college, so we shared the same educational background. In time, I received my surgical training in Cardiovascular and Thoracic Surgery from Yale University. Since then, I've performed over 5,000 open heart surgeries. I'm also honored to say I was inducted into The Beating Heart Hall of Fame. As we talked, I found Shane engaging and brilliant. I also learned that we had more in common than I had originally thought.

I quickly learned that Shane's journey was similar to mine. After performing thousands of coronary bypass operations, I finally came to understand that cholesterol lowering meds, diabetes drugs and low fat diets were harming my patients. I watched as countless heart attack victims lost their health to the misguided war on cholesterol and the use of prescription meds. When I spoke out to help my patients, I was scorned, labeled a quack and my career slandered in the media!

Regardless, I continued "confessing" what I had witnessed under the lights of my sterile operating room. I guided my patients toward better lifestyle habits and natural alternatives. Threatening my hospital's revenue stream, the medical license I was no longer using was officially revoked. From that point forward, I—like Shane—remained determined to "help people ditch their meds."

In 3 Worst Meds, he explains the real cause of heart disease with 100% accuracy. He shows us why cholesterol-lowering drugs are the biggest fraud in medical history and the vast harm they cause. But that's just the start. He has ominous warnings about many other so-called "blockbuster drugs."

Death by medicine has risen precipitously, year after year. In 2006 researchers found that prescribed medicine was the leading cause of death, more than cancer and heart disease. It's just gotten worse since then!

As the cover of this book indicates, we are dangerously hovering in "the red zone" for medication overdoses. Deaths are reaching 65,000 per year—a number impossible for most people to fathom. Adverse drug reactions (ADEs) and accidental medicine deaths are adding to the death toll. Without a doubt, modern medicine has become the biggest threat to our longevity. You're 9,000 times more likely to be killed by a doctor than a gun owner.

Doctors seem to have forgotten the first axiom of medicine: "Above all do no harm." If you're one of the 70% of Americans taking at least one prescription drug, you may be at risk for becoming a victim of the 3 worst meds.

Don't count on Big Pharma, the Food and Drug Administration (FDA), or your doctor to save you. The market for medicine is immensely profitable, which makes the temptation for lying about results too great. This is seen in aggressive prescribing habits of doctors who push the 3 worst meds, as well as the erroneous papers published in medical journals making meds appear safe and effective. The world has been conned.

A recent study showed that 90% of meds are prescribed for the wrong reason. Editors of the world's most prestigious medical journals—The *Journal of the American Medical Association* and *New England Journal of Medicine*—have stated that most of the medical research published today simply can't be trusted. Yet medication sales are skyrocketing to record highs, year after year.

The *British Medical Journal* published that two thirds of medical research is now sponsored by the drug industry. Medical journals—the go-to source for doctors to receive their information—have become accomplices, camouflaging the risks of top meds and even hiding the deaths that occur during clinical trials! Where does that leave us as medical consumers?

Life is billions of electro-chemical reactions in every single cell, brilliantly coordinated to form us into the physical beings that we are. One mishap and it's over. Who better than a chemist to explain how things work underneath the surface? Shane's intelligence, unique experience and ardent research allows him to separate the BS (bad science) or barnyard BS (i.e., the lies that Big Pharma tells us) from the truth, for our benefit.

For anyone who's been told that their life depends on meds, *3 Worst Meds* is a must-read—a life preserver in a tumultuous sea of lies and highly organized deceit. This book shows you a different route—one that will help you get off the medication treadmill so that you're not accidentally serving as an annuity to the medical industry, only to end up prematurely in a body bag.

DWIGHT LUNDELL, MD
Author of *Confessions of a Maverick Heart Surgeon and Iron Man*
Get it free at www.drlundellmd.com

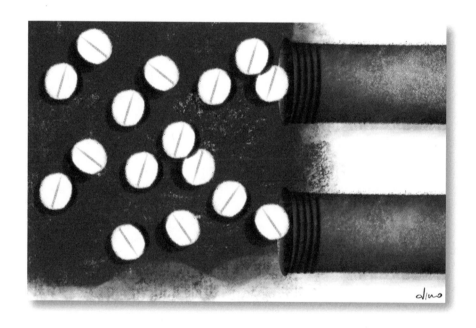

Your Health Is
Your Own Responsibility

*Sadly, over time, I've watched people die from things that could've been
easily avoided by ditching their meds. Using natural medicine and
adhering to healthy habits would have saved them . . . period.*

For over 25 years, I've been studying chemistry and medicine.
During that time, I've been astonished by the number of
unhealthy people who've told me they've "tried everything to be
healthy." Without exception, these are the same individuals who
throw their hands up in the air and insist, "Nothing works." God
himself could hand them the ultimate health solution on a silver
platter, and they'd still find reason to lament.

"Nothing works" is code for "I take zero responsibility for my
health and am just looking for the next target to blame." Don't
believe me? Think about this: how could anyone possibly have "tried
everything" in this massive, infinite universe? That's hubris . . . and
a physical impossibility.

I can't help but think these people never learned to grind. They
were taught to quit. Today, most people allow themselves to be programmed to lose. Everywhere you look, there's a sea of complacent
losers swimming in their own self-created misery—complaining

24/7 about their lives, yet can't be bothered to change a damn thing. (It's easier to bitch on social media and distract oneself with selfies, politics, and entertainment.)

My 11-year-old son, Blair, competed in a submission grappling jiu-jitsu tournament. After hitting a beautifully executed, double leg takedown in the first five seconds, he got caught in a guillotine choke. Amid hundreds of screaming parents, a tap out and quick loss looked imminent.

The guillotine is one of the simplest and most cunning of all chokes in grappling. Your neck gets firmly locked, noose-tight, inside your opponent's death grip. But if you can scrape up enough determination to keep trying, the guillotine has weaknesses to exploit.

Big Pharma currently has millions of Americans trapped in a prescription drug "guillotine." The industry knows most people will simply give up and "tap out" before they even come close to figuring shit out. Burdened by side effects from their current prescription drugs, most people will just take MORE meds to mask the negative outcomes, while enriching their pill masters' pockets. It's a never-ending spiral—one in which health inevitably declines.

But that doesn't have to be your fate. You're holding this book, which will open your eyes and inspire you to free yourself. I wrote 3 *Worst Meds* to help people just like you escape from Big Pharma's choke hold. Using it, you can ditch the deadly pills in orange bottles, save your precious money, and ultimately add quality years to your life.

Sadly, over time, I've watched people die from things that could've been easily avoided by ditching their meds. Using natural medicine and adhering to healthy habits would have saved them . . . period. They refused to read a simple book that could have shown them the way to freedom. They gave up and dutifully swallowed handfuls of meds until an early trip to the grave forced them to stop. Ironically, their meds were much riskier than the illness they were trying to beat.

While it's easy to point the finger at prescription drug companies and various diseases—it's ultimately the patient's own fault. For not giving a damn. For not educating themselves. For not taking the time to question, "Do I really need to swallow these pills?" If you take anything away from this book, know that your health is YOUR responsibility. I'm not victim-shaming anyone. I'm saying it's time to wake up and stop blindly trusting doctors and drug companies to YOUR health.

Every day people give themselves cancer, heart disease, and obesity by tolerating their own ignorance. They resort to whatever pills doctors feel like prescribing them. Not once do they stop to say, "I'm in charge of my own health." They never bother to look for healthier alternatives, nor are they willing to make simple healthy lifestyle changes.

Of course, Big Pharma loves this complacency! They're complicit in this charade—which is literally a mass poisoning via prescription meds. This trend of choking people with meds wouldn't occur without the willful ignorance that has become the norm in today's society. Swallowing unnecessary meds is the equivalent of tapping out early—it's giving up.

Pill pushers bank on your ignorance. The drug industry's business model of "profiting off those who give up" was devised long before any of us were born. Hell, most people aren't even aware they're suffocating from a Big Pharma Guillotine right now, as we speak. (If you're on ANY prescription drug—even hormonal birth control pills—then you're caught in a guillotine!)

Drug makers know the average American would rather take advice from a random drug ad than read a book. They know you'll probably run to a doctor before ever hitting the gym. They know people would rather scour drug ads in a trendy magazine before ever reading a damn food label.

If you take the time to educate yourself by reading 3 *Worst Meds*, you'll see that poor health is reversible. Like a guillotine choke, bad health has weaknesses to exploit. Signs of ill health show themselves years before it's "too late." And you ALWAYS have a choice. You have the power to change your own health even in ways that might seem miraculous—by using science combined with natural medicine.

You can change your fate long before your declining health becomes permanently "irreversible." Unless you're dead, keep fighting. Best of all, you don't need a single medication to do it. That's right—no thin piece of paper with sloppy handwriting to carry to your dutifully over-worked, stressed out pharmacist. No orange bottles stapled into a white paper bag. No side effects to endure. No co-pays. No meds, period.

Imagine a life free from all that shit.

Cinched up, Blair knew he was in deep water. His face turning fire engine red, he heard coaches hovering over the mat, yelling for his opponent to squeeze harder. Blair took one last breath to buy 30 seconds of time. This was his last-ditch effort to figure something out. Although he was losing air, he refused to give up.

He went into the "tripod" position. His hips stacked up high, his shoulder pressed the air out of his opponent, giving him a dose of his own medicine. Reaching behind his assailant's neck, Blair stacked hard enough to break the grip.

He was free! He could breathe. But he knew the fight had just begun, and his gas tank was on empty. Continuing to push on after you've already given it your all is how the battle is ultimately won.

Anyone can go to war when they're already winning. That's easy. Only a true champion has the drive and courage to dig deep and keeping fighting while smack in the middle of a devastating loss. When you do that, losing is only a temporary setback on the road to victory.

Most people regard this kind of victory in defeat as impossible. They refuse to keep fighting. They refuse to find a better way. They associate themselves with permanent loss.

I decided long ago never to waste a single second trying to help those people. Millions are genuinely searching for a way out, while leaving their excuses at the door—those are the people I'm here to serve.

If you aren't willing to read and fight to regain health and longevity, how is anyone supposed to help you? How will you know who to believe? How will you make life-changing decisions required for your own health and that of your family's health?

With little time left, Blair escaped. But ultimately, he didn't get his hand raised in victory. That's not what mattered. What mattered is that he walked away having learned a valuable life lesson—it's better to try and lose, than to NOT try at all and tap out. Because when you give up, you neither win nor live.

He'll carry this wisdom into his adult years. In time, as his character develops, he'll respect the daily effort required to never fear the fight. The meaning of sacrifice and the reason for it will always supersede mere winning and losing. That alone will prevent Blair from ever failing while insisting, "I've tried everything!"

Honestly, if any of my kids ever told me they "tried everything," they'd get a well-executed spanking. If I expect to raise kids who don't whine, act-out, or become liberal government slaves waiting for the next medical, insurance or welfare program handout, then it's mandatory that I enforce highly defined boundaries that teach my kids healthy discipline. Who the hell else will teach them?

Learning to never give up and fight is your insurance policy against failure. That drive can help you take a stand against poor health and pharmaceutical corruption that aims to hook you on meds for life.

That's part of why I wrote *3 Worst Meds*. I wanted to equip courageous fighters with the knowledge needed to live young without meds. Better than a book, it's a weapon—something you can use to win the battle for optimal health once and for all. This book will help you experience measurable results such as:

- Fat loss
- Increased energy
- Better mental outlook
- Enhanced libido
- Looking younger than your peers
- Preserved memory
- Total heart health
- Vaccine-free immunity
- An overall higher quality of life

Carefully Screened Natural Alternatives

In addition to exposing the 3 worst meds known to Western Medicine, I've also highlighted the forgotten and often hidden natural alternatives, where applicable. There are nine of them included! To ensure safety and efficacy, each recommendation comes with:

- Suggested dose
- Best time to take

As a chemist, I've also run dozens of quality control tests in my lab to verify that my supplement recommendations aren't contaminated. A single test can cost up to $5,000, which is far too costly for the average consumer to do on their own, especially when multiple products are involved.

My state-of-the-art testing methods are the same ones I used as a bench chemist for Big Pharma as well as my own company, The People's Chemist (www.ThePeoplesChemist.com). As part of my *Blue Diamond Series,* I've included all the test results free of charge in this book (see last chapter)! A matter of life and death, this type of razor-sharp laboratory precision is glossed over or even left out by doctors and online vitamin hucksters!

My methodology for testing purity and potency validates that each product is naturally sourced (botanical) and not made in a lab (synthetic), which causes undue side effects and detracts from health. I also carefully screen for impurities such as pesticides, heavy metals, preservatives, and microbes from viral or bacterial contamination. And finally, every product has been tested to ensure that it carries the active, medicinal ingredients—from nature— required for a measurable result! Who else can provide that deep level of verification that a supplement is of high quality?

You can also rest assured that all of my suggestions are free of any financial ties. In other words, I don't do affiliate marketing. Nobody can pay me to recommend a product. I either find it of quality, or I don't. Each referral is based on availability, purity, effectiveness, and safety. And although I do sell similar products that are held to a very high purity and potency standard as well (www.thepeopleschemist.com), I realize my products are not always available or affordable, and have therefore left them out of my tirade against the 3 worst meds.

The Three Worst Meds

The hardest part about writing 3 Worst Meds was choosing them. There are so many harmful meds on the market, it's like trying to decide who's worse—Hitler or Stalin?

Birth control, antidepressants, chemotherapy drugs, antibiotics, stimulants for ADHD (attention-deficit/hyperactivity disorder), anti-anxiety meds, insulin, and pain meds dominate most people's lives. Over 50% of the American population is medicated...almost to death. The accompanying weight gain, depression, loss of memory, butchered energy, decreased motivation, and dwindling zest for life are all explained by the use of today's mandated addiction to meds. Despite mile-long lists of side effects and decades of failure, doctors continue to present their prescription drugs as scientifically proven "solutions" to imminent health problems.

Painkillers are leading the charge in overdoses. Almost 200,000 Americans have died from addiction and overdose (see cover graph). For almost 40 years, manufacturers have made false claims insisting that, "despite widespread use of narcotic drugs in hospitals, the development of addiction is rare in medical patients with no history of addiction." Meanwhile, an estimated 65,000 patients per year will continue to lose their lives, and that estimate is climbing. In 2007, painkiller manufacturers pleaded guilty to federal criminal charges that they misled regulators, doctors, and patients about the risk of addiction associated with the meds. But this is just the tip of the iceberg.

Ultimately, the WORST meds are those that are prescribed for daily use, as if they were vitamins. These are:

1. Blood pressure meds
2. Cholesterol-lowering drugs
3. Aspirin

These 3 worst meds are pushed as daily requirements for healthy living—*that's what sets them apart from other deadly medicines.* Meanwhile, the mortality figures among users of these meds keeps climbing.

Of course, this book wouldn't be complete without a discussion of vaccines. As a father of four, I can't be silent or pretend to be blind to the risks of childhood shots and their blatantly false representations.

Glossed over in the media as mandatory and well-researched, today's vaccine science is being relayed to the laymen with fuzzy generalizations and a thin patina of goodness. When you look at it from the perspective of a chemist and a father, you find that most vaccine science is an intricate work of fiction infused with a myriad of falsehoods and even cover-ups. Therefore, I've included a bonus chapter separating fact from fiction. In doing so, I've outlined three reasons why my wife and I chose not to vaccinate our four children.

3 Worst Meds is your ultimate health solution delivered on a silver platter—a no-holds barred exposé that serves as a much-needed wake-up call. Offering safe alternatives and simple lifestyle habits that yield positive measurable results, this book is the springboard for a new way of life—a definitive guide to escaping Big Pharma's guillotine.

You'll learn how to bulletproof your cardiovascular system, strengthen your heart, open your arteries from inflammation, beat malaria, defend against rogue blood clots, boost your child's immune system, and so much more you won't find anywhere on the Internet. Using this information, you can ditch the meds before they sabotage your memory, weight, health, and longevity.

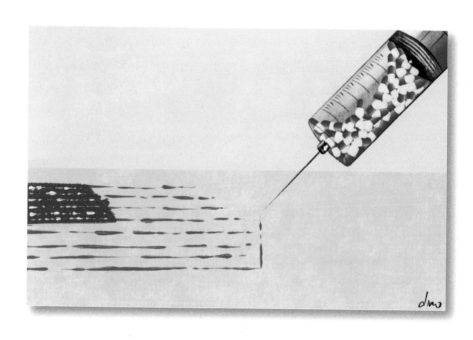

INTRODUCTION

Why I Abandoned
Western Medicine

If you dare to question your doctor about the prescriptions he doles out
to you, he'll most likely cite a bunch of medical journals as "references"
to substantiate his over-the-moon claims of safety and efficacy.

To understand my fury with the drug industry, it helps to know
my background. I was formerly a pharmaceutical drug chemist
paid to design drugs. As a medicinal chemist, I ignored my suspicion
for years that something wasn't right. Working for a large drug company, I became aware of an insidious and deliberate push to get each
and every American hooked on drugs, while at the same time bankrupting them. Who was behind this push? Big Pharma and the Food
and Drug Administration (FDA). Fresh out of graduate school, I
received a master's degree and was awarded graduate student of the
year. Then I scored a job with pharmaceutical titan, Eli Lily.

At first, it was a dream. Drug design paid well. It kept me com-
fortably isolated in a high-tech lab, fully equipped to help me bend
and twist matter at will. I enjoyed my work. The last thing I wanted
to think about was a sinister plot designed to sabotage the health and
wealth of millions. I didn't want to believe that using my chemistry
skills to design meds would contribute to this "mass poisoning"

underway, courtesy of Pharma and the FDA. But over time, my experience in the lab confirmed my suspicions as fact.

My passion for drug design initially arose from the miracle of emergency medicine—which is, by far, one of humankind's greatest scientific achievements. I'll be the first to admit that.

Sadly though, medicine is no longer reserved for emergency use. Instead, it's being used in a deadly game of profiteering, thanks to a pharmaceutical sales army that pushes unproven, toxic meds for everyday use—as if they were vitamins. Herein lies a story of deceit and my abandonment of modern medicine.

My First Assignment: Design a Drug to Stop Hot Flashes and Cancer

I was employed to design a new generation of Hormone Replacement Therapy (HRT) drugs, a class of drugs that includes Premarin, tamoxifen and raloxifene. They're erroneously prescribed to cool hot flashes among middle-aged women, as well as decrease the risk of cancer. This is when my doubts about modern medicine began sprouting up.

Initially, HRT meds were thought to work by blocking estrogen receptors. The hypothesis was that HRT meds could successfully put an end to hot flashes and cancer. Sounded good, right? As time progressed, we learned these drugs did just the opposite—they *activated* estrogen receptors and boosted cancer growth.

The Journal of the American Medical Association (JAMA) recognized this trend. In their article "Hormone Replacement Therapy in Relation to Breast Cancer," published in 2002, they wrote, "Our data add to the growing body of evidence that recent long-term use of HRT is associated with an increased risk of breast cancer and that such use may be related particularly to lobular tumors."[1]

My task was made clear: design HRT "knock-offs" that were effective without causing cancer. My attempt to design safer alternatives began with small alterations to the three-dimensional structure of tamoxifen. Pluck an atom here, add one there, and test it. Simple.

It was an everyday grind, but each new molecule and atomic re-arrangement brought new possibilities. During this process, one outcome remained the same: *no matter how the atoms were re-organized, they all caused cancer, just like their parent compound tamoxifen.* This is because all HRT drugs are inherently cancer-causing.

After one year of trial and error, the project was ended. I naively assumed that tamoxifen would be yanked from the market. To my surprise, access to tamoxifen and other HRT meds not only remained readily available—these drugs started being heavily marketed on TV. "What the fuck?!" I thought. Despite its ability to inflame and ignite cancer, tamoxifen remained the gold standard in breast cancer treatment.

That's when I realized something was seriously wrong. How does a drug that CAUSES cancer get promoted as a "cure" for cancer? How is it allowed to remain on the market, let alone be pushed as the gold standard cure? The irony was bizarre. It was impossible to wrap my head around. The evidence of tamoxifen's dangers was indisputable and heavily documented. The truth could have easily been proven in any experiment and in a court of law . . . so what the hell was going on?

As a young chemist, I was determined to better understand the irony. How could a toxic drug sail past the prestigious FDA approval process and make its way to the medicine cabinets of millions of people worldwide? Like a terrorist evading airport security, that's exactly what these meds are doing—bypassing everyone's radar. Thus began a lengthy process of pulling back the pharmaceutical curtain.

After a little digging, I discovered that "checkbook science," medical ghostwriting, and drug lobbying made up the Holy Trinity for drug approval and sales. Science was dead. Ethics were tossed out the window. The drug approval process itself was rigged by an insidious conflict of interest among the pharmaceutical industry and U.S. government. Shit. Was I really cut out to combat this glaringly obvious case of fraud? It would have been easier for me to just keep my mouth shut and continue collecting a paycheck. . . .

Soon I discovered tamoxifen was only the tip of the iceberg. Massive institutional corruption had seeped into the very fibers of the entire "healthcare system" (more accurately known as "sick care"). This corruption led to a slew of dangerous drugs being unleashed on the public, in the open market—with no one being held accountable.

Digging through piles of research papers and government documents made available by The Freedom of Information Act (FOIA), I learned that each and every risky medication is approved with the government's blessing. In fact, drug funding is siphoned directly from taxpayers (and insurance companies) to Big Pharma, courtesy of huge prescription med payouts made legal by The Bayh-Dole act. This made the tobacco industry look like saints.

In other words, the government was funding the very industry it was supposed to regulate. Meanwhile, drug companies paid that money right back to the government, in the form of lobbying and much more. Proof of this "revolving door" came from court documents showing that Big Pharma is completely shielded from liability, thanks to the U.S. government. Like an enabling parent, the government just looks the other way. No matter how many patients get cancer from tamoxifen or any other drug or vaccine, nobody in the drug industry will be held responsible. People will die and the industry will continue to profit outside of justice. [2]

Without any checks and balances in place, this pharmaceutical monster is free to roam as it pleases. The scam is so vast, I soon came to realize that few people would ever escape the corrupt culture that is now running modern day medicine.

. . . And it all starts with "checkbook science."

Checkbook Science: Paying for a Blockbuster Drug

Tamoxifen was originally developed in 1967 by British company Imperial Chemical Industries (ICI). Their pharmaceutical division was later spun off as AstraZeneca. Knowing that consumer demand drives drug approval, they—in partnership with the American Cancer Society—established "National Breast Cancer Awareness Month." This slick marketing campaign raised the fear level among women, which in turn raised the demand for tamoxifen.

Women worldwide began pushing for more choices in cancer drugs. Like puppets being manipulated on a string, they begged for the very drugs that would end up killing them. In Big Pharma language, that meant more drug approvals at a quicker rate. Artificial demand for tamoxifen had been successfully fabricated. Created out of thin air under the guise of "cancer awareness," this demand would later fuel big drug sales. Each and every year, this conditioned response among the public is reactivated, thanks to the self-serving pink ribbon campaigns. (When you see a pink ribbon "compassionately" posted on Facebook, you're seeing manipulation and greed.)

Unable to ignore the public outcry, the FDA found themselves backed into a corner. They were pressured into quickly approving a drug to treat cancer—never mind if the drug was safe or effective. Enter checkbook science. With the best "science" money could buy, AstraZeneca was standing by, ready to unleash mounds of fake positive research "proving" the safety and efficacy of tamoxifen.

Just like chemists can manipulate the properties of matter at will, Big Pharma can—and often does—manipulate scientific studies using checkbook science. They pay for the design and interpretation of chemistry research and clinical trials. This represents a gross conflict of interest that goes unnoticed today.

In order to hide the cancer-causing nature of tamoxifen, the maker simply stopped conducting all trials at five years. They called it a "5-year survive rate." Conveniently, five years is the minimum amount of time required for cancer to develop! Even proven cancer-causing substances like cigarettes take at least 5 years to confer cancer. Like a lazy housecleaner sweeping dirt under the rug, this strategy hid the cancer being caused by the estrogen-mimicking drug, tamoxifen! [3]

This kind of fraud still goes on today with shocking regularity among many other medications like vaccines and HIV meds, and especially with chemotherapy! I expose this in my book *Over-The-Counter Natural Cures Expanded*, which gives readers a cancer survival guide.

It gets worse. In 1992, tamoxifen evangelist Dr. Bernard Fisher, working for the National Cancer Institute (NCI) and AstraZeneca, received $68 million in federal money to assess whether the drug could prevent breast cancer. That's like asking a convicted child molester to assess the safety of a kindergarten class. In an effort to make tamoxifen appear safe and effective, Fisher failed to report falsified data and enrollment fraud. His actions cast an even worse stench over the study, resulting in his eventual termination as director. The smoke and mirrors of checkbook science made it appear that tamoxifen reduced breast cancer by 50%. In reality, it was an insignificant 1.3% absolute difference, which wasn't good enough for FDA approval. Meanwhile, independent studies showed that tamoxifen was CAUSING cancer at alarming rates. [4]

This is the essence of checkbook science—drug makers and the biotech industry as a whole twist the facts, data, and real science, in order to suit their agenda for patents, fast drug approval, and big sales. If a drug study doesn't make a proposed drug appear safe and effective, it's discarded or modified until it makes the drug look like the best thing since sliced bread.

By FDA standards, checkbook science isn't illegal. In fact, it's been going on since 1980. Known as the Bayh-Dole Act, U.S. law was amended in 1980 to reverse decades of government policy by allowing scientists, universities, and small businesses to patent and profit from discoveries they made through federally funded research.

In time, many of those discoveries have become nothing more than fraudulent science masquerading as medical advances. It's the best "science" money can buy. While this wasn't the original intent of the Bayh-Dole Act, it's the sad outcome of allowing institutions to keep the intellectual rights and patents to their tax-funded discoveries. [5]

Called the "Stealth Merger" by *The LA Times*, top scientists at the National Institutes of Health (NIH) now collect paychecks and stock options from the drug industry they serve. Once considered "an island of objective and pristine research, untainted by the influences of commercialization," the NIH has become corrupted by checkbook science.[6] To substantiate, we look to the following statistics:

- Dr. Stephen I. Katz, director of the NIH's National Institute of Arthritis and Musculoskeletal and Skin Diseases collected between $476,369 and $616,365 in fees from the drug industry over a 10-year period.

- From 1997-2002, Dr. John I. Gallin, director of the NIH's Clinical Center, received between $145,000 and $322,000 in fees and stock proceeds from the drug industry.

- Dr. Richard C. Eastman is the NIH's top diabetes researcher. As a consultant to the drug manufacturers in 1997, he wrote to the Food and Drug Administration (FDA) defending a product without disclosing his conflict of interest. His letter stated that the risk of liver failure from the given drug was "very minimal." Six months later, a patient taking the drug in an NIH study that Eastman oversaw, Audrey LaRue Jones, suffered sudden liver failure and died. An autopsy, along with liver experts, found that the drug had caused the liver failure.

- Dr. Ronald N. Germain, deputy director of a major laboratory at the National Institute of Allergy and Infectious Diseases, amassed more than $1.4 million of Big Pharma money in "consulting fees" from 1993 to 2003, plus stock options.

- Jeffrey Schlom, director of the National Cancer Institute's Laboratory of Tumor Immunology and Biology, received $331,500 in company fees over 10 years.

- Jeffrey M. Trent, who became scientific director of the National Human Genome Research Institute in 1993, reported receiving between $50,608 and $163,000 in industry consulting fees. He left the government in 2002.

NIH officials now allow more than 95% of the agency's top-paid employees to keep these "consulting" fees confidential. In fact, when it comes to disclosing financial conflicts of interest, the NIH is the most secretive agency in the U.S. government.

True science has been abandoned. Because of this, whenever you hear doctors regurgitate "result studies from peer reviewed papers," you can be damn sure it's checkbook science at work, not real science.

Once artificial demand was created using emotion-stirring pink ribbons, checkbook science painted the illusion that tamoxifen was safe and effective. Now the FDA just needed one study to approve the drug. They did that in record time—30 days flat! In fact, AstraZeneca hired advisors within Big Pharma to sit on the FDA review committee! Reviewing only 10% of the provided research, the committee, of course, gave tamoxifen the green light as a preventive cancer treatment for healthy women.

Aiming for wealth, not health, Big Pharma hit the financial bull's eye. Looked upon as the most effective treatment for breast cancer today, generic tamoxifen (Nolvadex) rakes in billions of dollars every year with few people noticing its "little cancer problem," as it became known in our lab.

Today doctors know very little, if anything, about how tamoxifen actually works in the body—or that it even causes cancer at all. That's because all of these facts have been buried by an avalanche of ghostwritten articles. Medical ghostwriters are genius at positioning tamoxifen as a novel anti-cancer drug, aromatase inhibitor, or whatever fancy concept the drug industry wants to sell it as!

Medical Ghostwriting: A Profession That's Paid to Lie

If you dare to question your doctor about the prescriptions he doles out to you, he'll most likely cite a bunch of medical journals as "references" to substantiate his over-the-moon claims of safety and efficacy. No doubt, whatever alleged piece of scientific writing he mentions will be dripping with the drug's so-called "benefits" and completely void of its reported side effects. These falsified studies are nothing more than expensive propaganda neatly crafted by ghostwriters and paid for by the same companies who make the medication.

A ghostwriter is someone who gets paid to be a drug industry cheerleader. They're paid to produce well-articulated, pseudoscientific writing. Once the final version is edited by Big Pharma, a top physician (opinion leader) signs off as author, even though that doctor never researched the topic or placed a finger on the keyboard. For their signature, they can fetch up to $30,000.

Polished and spit-shined, the completed paper is published in prestigious medical journals like *The New England Journal of Medicine* or *The Journal of the American Medical Association.* These writings are then used to sway doctors and the media into prescribing the industry's driblets of poison. Non-industry, unbiased published work—which does exist when you dig for it as I've done for

3 Worst Meds—is largely buried or forgotten. That's how tamoxifen slipped into the market. Ghostwriters hailed it as being wildly effective at preventing breast cancer. And doctors took the bait.

Meanwhile, independent studies—using real science, real data, and no conflicts of interest—have shown the opposite of what medical ghostwriting shows. A few people have spoken out.

David Roe, a former staff attorney with the Environmental Defense Fund and one of the authors of Proposition 65, intended to show Californians how to make informed decisions about protecting themselves from chemicals known to cause cancer, birth defects, or other reproductive harm. He insisted that tamoxifen be placed on the list of proven carcinogens for the state of California.

Citing independent studies from around the world, Roe showed a sixfold increase in uterine cancer among women treated with tamoxifen. This prompted the drug manufacturer to list a warning in the package insert that read, "An increased incidence . . . of endometrial cancer has been reported in association with Nolvadex treatment." The chairman of the state's scientific committee, epidemiologist Thomas Mack of USC, came forward to attest that the number of uterine or endometrial cancers caused by tamoxifen "is about as solid as it can get in humans." Regardless, the drug remained in the pharmacy as the go-to anticancer treatment for women worldwide. [7]

We have ghostwriting to thank for covering up this critical evidence. Ghostwriters always achieve the same outcome: make a drug look better than it is, so that doctors prescribe it, and patients receive bad drugs disguised as good medicine. This system allows individual writers to hide by staying anonymous, while forgoing any shred of responsibility for their actions. The result is massive carnage like the Vioxx™ body count—88,000 people died from taking Vioxx, which was hailed as "the safest painkiller," according to ghostwritten articles. [8] History is repeating itself today with opiates.

As deplorable as medical ghost authoring is, it's more common than you might think. It's part of the many insidious practices that make possible today's mass poisoning via prescription drugs. Dr. Jeffrey Drazen, editor for *The New England Journal of Medicine,* insisted that he couldn't find a single drug review author who didn't have obvious financial ties to drug companies. Dr. Richard Smith, editor of *The British Journal of Medicine* admitted that, "We are being hoodwinked by the drug companies. The articles come in with doctors' names on them and we often find some of them have little or no idea about what they have written." [9]

Are people seriously that desperate for a paycheck? You bet your ass they are. Ultimately, ghostwriting does more than just sell drugs. It's a tool used by scientists, doctors, and politicians to sell the myth of Western Medicine. If we actually paid doctors based on how healthy their patients are, all of them would be out of a job. Ghostwriting is the supreme manipulator, constantly working to coax the American public into swallowing meds—as if prescription drugs descended from the heavens for those lucky few who can afford them, courtesy of their insurance policy.

Dr. Leemon McHenry, a prominent PhD and professor of 30 years, told me in an interview, "Doctors who sign on these ghostwritten articles are guilty of fraud, of corrupting science and polluting the scientific record with misreporting of data."

The Emperor Has No Clothes

Unfortunately, despite the outcry from a few informed individuals, ghostwriting is still working. It's fooling nearly everyone. Consuming 50% of the world's total supply of prescription drugs, Americans form lines at the pharmacy like red ants at a picnic table. Without question, they "ask their doctor if the latest drug is right for them." This canned script is encouraged more than thinking for oneself. Newly devised screening programs for prostate cancer, "pre-diabetes," and breast cancer are all designed to encourage patients to ask this unintelligent question—"Is this drug right for me?" By design, the question is flawed. It's meant to lead to one obvious outcome—to get as many people as possible medicated - a term known to drug industry insiders as disease inflation. (It's the art of making people fearful of disease—invented illness or otherwise—so they can sell more meds.)

The fact that so many people are fooled is reflective of the childhood tale, "The Emperor Has No Clothes." In that story, two sneaky weavers promised the emperor a new set of clothes. They handed him an "invisible" gown, which he put on without question. People gathered around town, whispering and smirking at an obviously naked emperor who acted as though he was clothed. Nobody dared to speak up. Due to embarrassment—and not wanting to offend the emperor or lose their jobs—the adults stayed silent. Everybody was afraid of looking dumb, save for a loud-mouthed child who had no filter. They called out the obvious: "He's not wearing anything!"

Meanwhile, the drug industry is naked. Here's the truth: you have more control over your health than you realize. Simple healthy habits can erase virtually all symptoms of poor health. Your body is the best healer.

Regardless, most doctors default to taking the easy route - meds. They chirp, "The benefits outweigh the risks." We've been hearing this warble as far back as the 1950's, even as the so-called "wonderdrug" thalidomide was robbing children of their appendages.

Today, ghostwriting has successfully:

- Hooked children under 2 years of age on psychiatric meds
- Made grown men fear cholesterol
- Produced massive opiate addiction and deaths
- Shoved blood pressure pills down the throats of anyone over 30 years old
- Turned teens into doctor-approved meth-heads via ADHD meds
- Drugged our teen girls with cancer-causing birth control pills
- Increased women's use of psychoactive drugs—even during pregnancy

This shit has got to stop. As a chemist seeing the disparity between medical fact and fiction among doctors, I had to talk with an actual ghostwriter. That's when I found Dr. Linda Logdberg.

A former ghostwriter, she has a bachelor's degree from the University of Michigan, an MA in psychology from UCLA, and an MSW from the University of Michigan in Ann Arbor. She also has a PhD in neuroanatomy from UCLA. She has been a writer for more than 22 years (formerly publishing research reports under the name "Linda A. Paul").

She told me personally that a high salary, interesting work, convenience and flexibility, and a belief that she was helping sick people—were all compelling reasons for her to be a ghostwriter. Plus, she had three children to take care of.

Eventually though, Linda began noticing the industry was involved with a slew of dirty deals. After realizing her ghostwriting was nothing more than "marketing masquerading as science" (her words), she quit.

"Pharma is unworthy of trust: evidence from many sources reveal these companies to be focused on the bottom line only," she told me. Citing "fraud in authorship," she explained that "medical researchers rarely informed the public on the pitfalls of drugs. Instead, ghostwriters were crafting sales pitches for scientific publication and hired doctors moonlighting as the authors."

Writing for the the *British Medical Journal,* Vera H. Sharav, President of the Alliance for Human Research Protection (AHRP), warned the scientific community, "Since the 1990s editors have known (or should have) that [pharma] industry's influence was penetrating journals not only directly (through advertising) but indirectly—by planting favorable reports often written by professional ghostwriters but 'authored' by influential leaders in their field. Academic scientists traded their influence for cash, penning their names to biased, ghostwritten reports of trials they did not conduct, and whose source data they did not analyze. Others, constrained by contractual publication restriction agreements with the sponsoring company, published fraudulent reports based on partial data findings. As two thirds of medical research is now sponsored by industry, the most influential ("high impact") medical journals have become accomplices, camouflaging the commercial nature of industry promotional reports." [10]

Fortunately, a few leading medical journals are still publishing valuable, independent work that questions the safety and efficacy of modern medicine. It's just a matter of knowing how to differentiate fake ghostwritten work from genuine research. I've spelled out these critical differences in *3 Worst Meds*. All references in this book are verifiable. The published results have been duplicated independently by other scientists. If the validity of ghostwritten articles isn't thoroughly questioned, this form of fake communication will continue being used as the primary tool for swindling the public. Meanwhile, ghostwriting will sway the U.S. government into approving even more risky meds via drug lobbying.

Drug Lobbying—The Revolving Door

Lobbying (verb): To try to influence the thinking of legislators or other public officials for or against a specific cause: lobbying for stronger environmental safeguards; lobbied against the proliferation of nuclear arms.

I thought I was getting paid well as a new drug chemist. I was driving a brand new PT Cruiser (my wife hated it), had $15,000 in stock options, and was offered a $10,000 incentive to buy a new house. Heck, if I was really good, I would get a $4,500 raise after a year, which equated to a weekly burrito at Chipotle, with guacamole (which is extra), Mountain Dew included. I felt like I had "made" it. But after taking a closer look at the real drug profits being made, I realized I wasn't even making pennies on the pharmaceutical dollar.

Obscene amounts of drug profits were going to the pharmaceutical titans, their shareholders, and even to the FDA. That's right— rather than being funded solely by taxpayers, our drug administration was (and still is) being paid by the very industry it's supposed to regulate.

This is legal, courtesy of the Prescription Drug User Fee Act (PDUFA). Today the Center for Drug Evaluation and Research (CDER) at the FDA is dependent on drug companies for nearly half of its funding via the PDUFA. Prior to 1992 the government agency was funded and beholden to taxpayers. Today, it gets its lion's share of profits directly from Big Pharma via reviews, thanks to the PDUFA. That's great for Big Pharma and bad for patients. This questionable stream of income is the glue that binds the FDA to its drug lobbyists, while further influencing drug approval more than actual science does.

Drug lobbying greases the "FDA revolving door" and blurs the line between the drug industry and the U.S. government. If both entities profit from the sales of drugs, then there's simply no distinction between the two. One cannot be trusted to regulate the other.

According to a report by the Center for Public Integrity, congressmen are outnumbered two to one by lobbyists for the pharmaceutical industry. Many are later put onto the government payroll and vice versa. Total pharmaceutical lobbying in 2009 came to a whopping $267,893,947. That's enough money to feed 502 million starving African children. Instead, it pays the drug approval pipeline via 450 lobbying organizations, 1,743 lobbyists, and 1,113 revolvers (congress and senior congressional staffers who revolve in and out of the private and public sectors). Quite frankly, this is what kept tamoxifen on the market—drug lobbyists who profited from tamoxifen sales convinced government officials to let the drug stay there.[11]

One Nation Under Drugs

If stacked in cash, annual pharmaceutical profits would occupy two thousand stacks of bills. Each stack would be as high as the Empire State Building! You'd have more stacks of money than there are tall buildings in Los Angeles, and not enough people to guard them.

Today global revenues from prescription drugs are nearing the trillion dollar mark, year after year. The US takes the largest bite out of the pharmaceutical pie, consuming $300.3 billion in prescriptions annually.

With the collusion of the FDA, Big Pharma is now halfway to its goal of swindling the entire country into drug dependence. Today, America is a cult under the influence of Big Pharma, the U.S government, and Wall Street. We truly are "one nation under drugs."

For almost a hundred years, the masses have been exposed to pharmaceutically-funded mass education and TV without being taught a single shred of truth about preventive health and the risks of meds. Approximately 150 million Americans (just under half the country's population) are now taking one or more prescription drugs per month, with 37% of those over 60 years old taking five or more! And nobody is healthy. Just look around.

Flawed FDA approval, Big Pharma, and modern medicine are man's biggest threats. Together, government and industry have created a drug dealing, business model that's robbing every man, woman, and child in its path of life, liberty, and the pursuit of happiness. This profit-hungry machine has no checks or balances and no conscience, which makes it poised to become humanity's biggest threat.

If not checked, many physicians will become de facto pharmaceutical foot soldiers. Acting as the Praetorian guards of Big Pharma, they'll believe any propaganda served up from ghostwriting and checkbook science. In the words of Voltaire, *"Those who can make you believe absurdities, can make you commit atrocities."*

This age-old wisdom confirms what I've written in this book. Doctors are required to take an oath of, "First do no harm." But if they're unaware of the influences driving the drug approval process and corresponding drug sales, then their oath is meaningless. They might as well be crossing their fingers behind their back, like children.

As a chemist for a drug company, I had to face the cold, hard facts: Western Medicine has become a billion dollar empire not by relying on keen science, but rather by using corruption and deceit. The end result has been "One Nation Under Drugs" with slavery and sickness for all. Nobody on meds is free. You can't be healthy and on meds at the same time. Period. This subjugation of the population has resulted in a standard of health in America whereby sick care is disguised as "health care."

Each year, prescription drugs (used as prescribed) kill an estimated 105,000 people—on top of another 65,000 overdose—more casualties than the Vietnam, Afghanistan, and Iraq wars combined. This blatant attack on human life happens thanks to voluntary compliance or as I call it, *willful ignorance*. Most of us want to blame Big Pharma, doctors, and the government. But this blindness and myopic thinking hides the real question: "Are we really any healthier by taking all these meds?" For the sake of your own health (and life), it's up to you to ask this question—because clearly the "professionals" won't bother.

The answer to this question would shut down labs all across the world. Wall Street would take a much-needed pay cut. The government would have to find new scams to generate money. The system that aims to medicate us all to death would crumble overnight.

F%@k This . . . I Quit

Disgusted, I couldn't allow myself to be an accomplice any longer. Outside of an emergency, meds are the problem, not the solution. The science proves it. This truth continues to be the driving motivation for all the work I do. I'd miss the lab, but not the lies.

I gave my one-year notice, then spent the following year prepping for my departure. (I would have quit sooner—but if you quit without notice, you lose your stock options, which I needed.) At the time, my daughter Lily was a year old. I had an inflated car loan, along with typical family bills. My bank balance showed $14,000 from the initial signing bonus I'd received as a young, motivated chemist. Naively, I thought I had "plenty."

My first step was to shed the car payment. When I called the repo guys to come get my PT Cruiser, my wife was ecstatic. (She thought it was an extreme eye sore.) I replaced it with the smooth-running engine of a 250cc Honda Skyhawk motorcycle. I got it for $1,400. We were down to $12,600.

For the next four months—November through February—I rode that motorcycle to work, fulfilling my remaining duties at work. It was a 25-minute commute one way. We lived in snowy Denver, Colorado. The trickiest part was ignoring my urge to press the breaks over the ice patches. (I always waved to the guys in their warm SUVs looking at me in disbelief.) I needed a leather jacket and a helmet. My balance quickly dwindled to $12,400.

Planning a move to the same town where my wife and I had met, I rented a moving truck and a new home in Durango, Colorado. Barely moved in, our funds had sunk quickly. We were well below the $10,000 mark.

Lea-Ann was getting nervous. She started cutting hair to keep us afloat. For years, we shared a car, exercised with a medicine ball in the garage (Google my "18 Minute Workout"), and got gas money from her parents on a couple occasions while we visited. Meanwhile, I started a blog (ThePeoplesChemist.com) where I taught people how to ditch the meds. My brand became the antithesis of what people are normally told. Unfortunately for me, helping people ditch their meds didn't pay well. . .

A few people started listening along the way. And then a few more. Regrettably, I was up against a powerful monster. Checkbook science, ghostwriting, and pharmaceutical lobbying had successfully hooked most people on the 3 worst meds. I was determined to show as many people as possible the truth, which you now hold in your hands. Take it or leave it.

This book is proof that my early suspicions as a bench chemist for Pharma were true. An insidious and deliberate push to get each and every American hooked on drugs, while at the same time bankrupting them, does in fact exist. Today that push has grown into a forceful shove that starts at birth with a barrage of vaccines. From the time they squeeze out of the womb, infants are pummeled with shots, a sinister welcome gift into "One Nation Under Drugs." What happens in the hospital is a foreshadowing of what's to come in life.

With the reckless voracity of a school of hungry pirañas in bloodied water, Big Pharma parades the world behind a mask of philanthropy and health. Meanwhile, it disregards science and the precious lives of billions of people worldwide. Those controlling this profit-driven, prescription drug conveyor belt should hold some sort of record for having the most reckless disregard for human life. If Big Pharma's and the FDA's onslaught is allowed to continue, it will silently kill more people than all wars and genocides combined.

Introduction Bibliography

(1) Chen CL, Weiss NS, Newcomb P, Barlow W, White E. Hormone replacement therapy in relation to breast cancer. *Journal of the American Medical Association.* 2002 Feb 13;287(6):734-41.

(2) Transparency International. Pharmaceuticals and Healthcare Programme. *Corruption in the Pharmaceutical Sector Diagnosing the Challenges.* Published June 2016. ISBN: 978-1-910778-55-5

(3) Holly L. Howe, Phyllis A. Wingo, Michael J. Thun, Lynn A.G. Ries, Harry M. Rosenberg, Ellen G. Feigal, Brenda K. Edwards. Annual Report to the Nation on the Status of Cancer (1973 Through 1998), Featuring Cancers With Recent Increasing Trends. Journal of the National Cancer Institute (2001) 93 (11): 824-842.

(4) Altman, Lawrence. Researcher Falsified Data in Breast Cancer Study. *The New York Times.* March 14, 1994.

(5) Markel, Howard. Patents, Profits, and the American People—The Bayh–Dole Act of 1980. *New England Journal of Medicine.* August 29, 2013.

(6) David Willman. Stealth Merger: Drug Companies and Government Medical Research David Willman. *LA Times.* December 07, 2003.

(7) Ju-Yin Chen, Shou-Jen Kuo, Yung-Po Liaw, Itzhak Avital, Alexander Stojadinovic, Yan-gao Man, Ciaran Mannion, Jianlian Wang, Ming-Chih Chou, Horng-Der Tsai, Shou-Tung Chen, and Yi-Hsuan Hsiao. Endometrial Cancer Incidence in Breast Cancer Patients Correlating with Age and Duration of Tamoxifen Use: a Population Based Study. *Journal of Cancer.* 2014; 5(2): 151–155.

(8) Saul, Stephanie. Celebrex Commercial, Long and Unconventional, Draws Criticism. *New York Times.* April 10, 2007.

(9) Barnett, Antony. Revealed: how drug firms 'hoodwink' medical journals. *The Guardian.* December 7, 2003.

(10) Vera H. Sharav. President, Alliance for Human Research Protection (AHRP). Journals Must Exercise Their Authority as Gatekeepers. *British Medical Journal.* 2006;333:0-f.

(11) Ismail, M. Asif. *A record year for the pharmaceutical lobby in '07. Washington's largest lobby racks up another banner year on Capitol Hill.* The Center for Public Integrity. June 24, 2008 Updated: 12:19 pm, May 19, 2014.

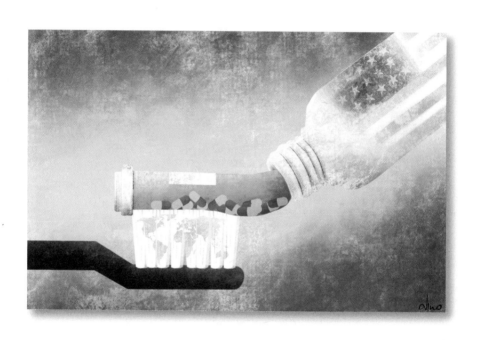

1

Who Needs
Blood Pressure Pills?

When swallowed, this weight-inflating class of meds
works by slowing the heart rate to elicit
a lower blood pressure reading.

When I travel I always visit a new grappling gym. Whereas some people like to visit landmarks, I enjoy learning new jiu-jitsu techniques from some of the world's greatest trainers. (Plus, it makes me work harder when everyone on the mat is trying to kill the new guy)

Landing in Scottsdale, Arizona, I found Fight Ready. It's home to many MMA pros like Olympic gold medalist wrestler Henry Cejudo and UFC star Frankie Saenz. Wrestling is coached by Thom Ortiz, a 3x All-American, 3x PAC-10 Coach of Year from ASU and Hall of Fame inductee, founder of The World Fighting Federation (WFF) and undefeated MMA fighter.

I was lucky enough to train with all of them. Afterwards, the topic of medications came up. (I can't go anywhere without hearing about someone getting screwed by their meds.) Thom shared how he was almost killed by blood pressure drugs.

As his high blood pressure crept up, his doctor insisted he was at greater risk for heart attack and stroke. In the same breath, he prescribed Thom blood pressure meds. (Keep in mind, Thom was only 42 years old at the time.) Trusting his doctor, he complied and dutifully began taking the meds. In time, his body began deteriorating.

A competitor at 155 pounds, Thom was mortified as the scale soon hit 205 pounds. While on meds, he became lethargic and depressed. Grappling, exercise, sex, and essentially everything else that's important—all took a backseat to his new, doctor-mandated drug use. Diet and exercise failed to help.

Thom's entire well-being and identity were stolen—all because of one fucking blood pressure pill. He had no idea that blood pressure meds (known as beta blockers) would slow his metabolism! When swallowed, this weight-inflating class of meds works by slowing the heart rate to elicit an artificially lower blood pressure reading. The less pumping the heart does, the less pressure there is . . . which also means less oxygen distribution and less nutrient distribution throughout the body. As the body gets starved of vital nutrients, it goes into crisis mode and begins packing on the weight, preparing for a famine. Doctors today somehow think this is healthy.

Simultaneously, beta blockers also throw hormones out of balance. Fat storage begins to take precedence over fat burning. No matter how hard you try, you can't lose weight while you're on blood pressure meds, due to this insidious blockade of metabolic function.

Fortunately, Thom saved himself and ditched the meds. Thanks to a naturopathic doctor, he learned the dangers of blood pressure pills and trashed them. His weight rebounded and today he's med-free.

Not everyone's that lucky. For most people, taking blood pressure pills just leads to more pills. It causes a prescription drug landslide, where side effects show up—and they begin taking additional meds to offset the side effects of the original meds. And on and on. This chemical assault to the body causes people to lose energy and motivation. Their belly starts pushing bigger belt sizes and their testosterone bottoms out like a sunken ship.

In time, blood pressure meds cause Type II diabetes, heart disease, then cancer, or all of the above. This is when doctors go completely nuts and start prescribing even more meds—metformin, aspirin and other blood thinners, and even the worst possible drug, insulin! It's like a merry-go-round, always getting a new drug when they return to the doctor's office with side effects from the previous prescription.

"The emperor has no clothes." In other words, the "blockbuster" meds being prescribed by the doctor aren't working!

In any other profession, this kind of "expert" would be fired or jailed for doing such egregious harm to the client. Not in Western Medicine. Doctors are rewarded for piling on more and more meds.

Meanwhile, patients die young, Big Pharma gets rich. Wall Street wolfs buy more jets. The sales strategy is repeated.

This tragedy is occurring in broad daylight, all over the country . . . and nobody is doing shit about it. Why? Because this deadly sales trajectory is funneling massive profits to Big Pharma and a portion us used to paint a benevolent portrait of Big Pharma in the media worldwide.

Currently, drug company-funded research insists that 70 million Americans should be on blood pressure meds. Paid experts are encouraging and enabling people to take these drugs. Cardiologist Dr. Cam Patterson, Chief Operating Officer at the New York-

Presbyterian Hospital/Weill Cornell Medical Center insists that, "Many blood pressure medicines are relatively cheap and cost effective. This might be a way to significantly reduce the consequences of high blood pressure and improve cardiovascular health without breaking the bank, for once."[1]

In September of 2016, the Centers for Disease Control and Prevention (CDC) announced that "Poor blood-pressure control puts 5 million older Americans at risk." In their pharmaceutically-funded propaganda piece, they insisted that millions of "Medicare enrollees age 65 and older are not taking their blood pressure medicine properly, increasing their risk of heart disease, stroke, kidney disease, and death."[2]

This kind of marketing tripe is part of what allows the "mass poisoning by meds" to occur legally, in broad daylight. But as you'll soon learn, this is just a slick ploy for scaring perfectly healthy people into taking meds. After all, the one suggestion made to correct high blood pressure was to "take your blood pressure medicine as prescribed," said CDC Director Tom Frieden, MD, MPH. Could the conflict of interest be any more obvious? Why not suggest healthy lifestyle changes and proven natural alternatives?

For most people, it's time to get the hell off blood pressure meds. Your doctor's assurances that "you have a history of hypertension in your family" and "lower is better," are nothing more than contrived sales pitches for meds.

Collect all the memorized quotes from pharmaceutically compliant doctors, and you'd have the biggest pile of medical bullshit since they prescribed heroin for coughing, or Coca-Cola for headaches. (They also used to prescribe lobotomies for psychiatric patients, thalidomide for morning sickness, and birth control for cramping. WTF?) The pile of bullshit is so high, most people born today don't even know it's there. Like a frog sitting complacently in water as it boils, it's just a permanent fixture among the status quo.

I've been warning people against blood pressure meds for fifteen years. Those who have listened to me are enjoying a life free of side effects and a perfectly healthy cardiovascular system. (And they're out-living their peers by a landslide.) Meanwhile, millions of brain-dead doctors and media pundits continue to rationalize the wanton use of blood pressure meds for whatever bogus reason they can find.

Sadly, the average American believes every shit piece of advice spoon-fed to them via the radio, television, and social media. They're conditioned to want meds. When they suffer from inevitable side effects, they ask for more! Society panders to this institutionalized, psychotic mindset.

In addition to hearing Thom's story, I got an email just hours after leaving the gym. A fellow pilot, Roger, told me he was on the verge of losing his pilot's license due to poor health caused by prescription drugs. He wrote:

> "I too am a skeptical person when it comes to ads, but the fact that your ad was in the AOPA magazine and by a fellow pilot made me think your natural blood pressure cure might be credible."

> "I am 58. About 5 years ago while getting my third class medical, the examiner said my blood pressure was getting a little high and suggested I talk to my personal doctor about what to do. So being a little naive and trusting, I went to the doctor and was immediately prescribed meds with a follow-up in a month. Still trusting, I went back and now was prescribed beta-blockers and statins for my high cholesterol."

"Another month passes and I feel that life as I knew it must be gone, as I feel so old and weak. Five years pass and with 20 pounds gained, now the doctor says I have adult-onset diabetes. Now I feel terrible all the time and am becoming even weaker. This last Christmas my 78-year-old parents visited. I noticed my father, yes 78, has more energy than me. Something is not right!"

"To make a long story short, your website and book which I purchased saved my life. Now with your recommendations I am completely off the poison. I truly feel 15 years younger in just 3 months. This is no gimmick and really works. Thank You, Thank You, Thank You!!"

When I followed up with Roger, I had to know if he got back in the pilot's seat. Sure enough, just like Thom had ditched his meds in favor of living young and grappling, Roger was happy to report he was now living his dreams and continuing to fly the friendly skies! And it was all done by simply getting the hell off meds.

What Should My Blood Pressure Be?

Simply being alive raises blood pressure (BP). You don't necessarily need medications to adjust it. Unfortunately though, far too many people have been drugged by their doctors—or even dentists—to curb the natural rise in blood pressure.

This is a dangerous game of roulette. Understanding what a normal, healthy BP is will help you make better decisions about medications and their natural alternatives.

Long-term blood pressure is controlled primarily by the kidneys via a chemical cascade known as the renin-angiotensin system. This was discovered in 1898 with studies made by scientists who found that they could manipulate blood pressure with kidney extracts.[3]

Decades later, chemists from Eli Lilly in Indianapolis and the Medical School of the University of Buenos Aires, Argentina, isolated the chief compound responsible for raising blood pressure. They named it angiotensin. Today, this kidney specific molecule is the primary target for many blood pressure controlling meds. Block it and blood pressure will drop.

The body has many incalculable feedback mechanisms that promote the healthy rise and fall of blood pressure. Exercise, stress, passion, excitement, obesity, smoking, and even the immune system can all cause temporary spikes in blood pressure. Sometimes these are normal; sometimes they're not so normal. The trick is deciding when to intervene.

For example, various emotions of excitement and fear (perhaps from sitting in a dental chair) can spur the arteries and veins to expand and narrow. This can result in short-term spikes in blood pressure. Anything that increases the heart rate, blood volume, or the expanding and narrowing of arteries and veins can increase blood pressure. Hell, even my swearing can raise your blood pressure.

All too often though, the smallest jump in blood pressure becomes the perfect excuse to hook patients on daily meds. This is when it gets risky.

During the first year of life, the average BP for an infant is 100/70. The top number is known as systolic and represents the amount of pressure placed on the arteries when the heart contracts. The bottom number is known as diastolic and represents the pressure when the heart relaxes.

If you're lucky enough to age, your BP will continue to rise. This is a normal, healthy process. Remember that. In most cases of rising blood pressure, there's nothing to fear. It's usually just a response to the body's increased need for oxygen, nutrients, or energy.   .

For decades, Big Pharma has been making sweeping generalizations about blood pressure levels. They push everyone to drive their blood pressure lower and lower, suggesting a uniform systolic (top number) of 120. These guidelines of "lower is better" have been at war with scientific evidence, which proves that "lower is not better" as we age. In other words, high blood pressure—defined as anything over 140/80—is actually healthy as we age. It's NOT a death sentence! Evidence for this truth was uncovered over a century ago!

In fact, it was first outlined in *Circulation of the Blood: Men And Ideas*. Cardiovascular research pioneers Fred Akbar Mahomed, Clifford Allbutt, and Henri Huchard demonstrated from 1874 to 1893 that hypertension (i.e., high blood pressure) may occur without overt renal disease and may even be present *before* hardening of the arteries or blockage.[4]

Think about it. That means rising blood pressure is not a sign of illness, whatsoever. These scientists coined the term "essential hypertension" to describe the elevation of blood pressure as a normal, compensatory reaction to healthy aging. Ever since then, this same research has been duplicated and observed by scientists . . . while being entirely ignored by Big Pharma and the media.

In a 1912 speech to the Glasgow Southern Medical Society, Sir William Osler made the following statement about high blood pressure being associated with atherosclerosis: "In this group of cases it is well to recognize that the extra pressure is a necessity—as purely a mechanical affair as in any great irrigation system with old encrusted mains and weedy channels. *Get it out of your heads, if possible, that the high pressure is the primary feature, and particularly the feature to treat.*"

These early biological observations were the eventual basis for scientists to discourage the development of blood pressure drugs. In 2016, *The British Medical Journal* published findings that confirmed these early sentiments and warnings. Independent researchers in Sweden conducted a systematic review and meta-analyses guided by recommendations of the Cochrane Collaboration. Comparing about 74,000 patients lowering their blood pressure with meds, they concluded, "This systematic review and meta-analyses confirms if systolic blood pressure is less than 140 mm Hg, we found no benefit, but potential harm, with an increased risk of cardiovascular death."[5]

The harm they reported came from prescription drug side effects. This represents a classic story of the "cure" being worse than the so-called disease. Not only did this put a spotlight on the dangers of meds, it also proved that essential hypertension (that which is over 140 systolic) is not a valid reason for drug use—but rather, an indication of healthy living as we age. The body is simply maximizing its ability to deliver more oxygen and nutrients as needed.

Therefore, when so-called promoters of Western Medicine assert that we ALL need to have blood pressure lower than 140/80, they're giving horrible advice that could kill you. It's nothing more than a sales ploy. As a former pharmaceutical chemist, I saw this message being pushed far too many times. To further disprove the "lower is better" dogma of the medical community, just look at lifespan among those who adhere to it. If high blood pressure were truly dangerous, then lowering it with hypertension drugs would increase longevity. But the opposite is true as I showed in my book, *Over-The-Counter Natural Cures Expanded.*

Studies in older people found that those who reduced their systolic pressure to less than 140 fared no better than those who reduced it to between 140 and 160. In fact, when studying 80-year-olds on blood pressure meds, *The Journal of American Geriatrics* reported that, "In a complete population of individuals with hypertension in primary care aged 80 and older treated under guidance to achieve SBP [systolic blood pressure] less than 150 mmHg, *greater mortality* was found over 11.9 years of follow-up in those with SBP of less than 135 mmHg."[6]

Worse, the medicated patients suffered undue side effects . . . like always. These included obesity, diabetes, kidney disease, and cancer as a direct result of using drugs like beta blockers, ACE-inhibitors and calcium channel blockers. Quality of life was eroded exponentially, despite the "doctor approved" lower-is-better numbers.

In an interview with *The New York Times*, Dr. Suzanne Oparil, director of the Vascular Biology and Hypertension Program at the University of Alabama at Birmingham School of Medicine affirmed the risk by saying, "Medications that lower blood pressure can have effects that counteract some of the benefits. The mantra of blood pressure experts in the past has been that lower is better. Recent studies don't seem to support that."

In that same article titled, "Hypertension Guidelines Can Be Erased," *The New York Times* wrote, "New guidelines suggest that people over 60 can have a higher blood pressure than previously recommended before starting treatment to lower it. The advice, criticized by some physicians, changes treatment goals that have been in place for more than 30 years."[7]

In sum, past, previous and current research supports the early theory of chemists and doctors who had their head on straight—that prescription drug side effects far outweigh the benefits of using meds to lower blood pressure. In general, it's completely natural for the first number (systolic) to be 100 plus our age. Diastolic pressure has shown no correlation to early death. But if it goes to 100, you may or may not have poor kidney health. Otherwise, rising blood pressure is simply essential hypertension. It's the body's way of delivering more oxygen and nutrients. The exception to the rule would be if you have rising blood pressure coupled to obesity, heart disease or Type II diabetes.

If you have any of these conditions, in addition to rising blood pressure, then it's no longer essential high hypertension. It's a warning sign of poor health. At best, your unhealthy lifestyle habits are eroding away your longevity and you need to make a change. At worst, it could be a sign of coronary events, stroke, heart failure, and end-stage renal disease (ESRD). That's when your doctor will start throwing a barrage of blood pressure meds at you such as beta blockers, ACE inhibitors, and calcium channel blockers. Before you start following doctor's orders, you had better know the risks of each of these meds. (Just remember Thom the grappler and Roger the pilot and how blood pressure meds butchered their health!)

How Blood Pressure Meds Harm You

Currently, three types of blood pressure meds are commonly prescribed—beta blockers, calcium channel blockers, and ACE-inhibitors. Although they all aim to achieve "better" (i.e., lower) BP numbers, each one works in a different way. Understanding their "mechanism of action" highlights their dangers and overt toxicity.

Beta-blockers are the most common blood pressure meds. The name refers to their ability to block a family of receptors in the body known as "beta-receptors." They're responsible for controlling heart beat, fat metabolism, and energy.

When activated, beta-receptors trigger increases in heart rate, thanks to naturally produced compounds from the adrenal glands. This ensures that your heart rate increases in response to activity. But that's not all. Flipped on, they also shuttle fat into your cells' fuel furnace—the mitochondria—to create an abundance of energy. Hence, beta-receptors are a primary activator of fat loss.

If you cover up these life-activating receptors, you will also slow heart rate, fat metabolism, and energy production. (Just like when you take your foot off the gas, your car will eventually slow down.) This is measured as a drop in blood pressure. But in time, this receptor-shielding throws hormones out of whack. The body then becomes ripe for cancer, heart disease, and Type II diabetes. Still, for almost 50 years, doctors have been misinterpreting the unhealthy drop in blood pressure as a "healthy" outcome!

To avoid the side effects of beta-blockers, some doctors opt for ACE-inhibitors. ACE-Inhibitor stands for angiotensin-converting enzyme. Designed from snake venom, these drugs relax the arteries—but they do it so damn much that heart failure becomes a real and present danger among users. *The Pharmaceutical Journal* warned doctors, "While most hypertensive patients could cope with feeling a little dizzy, the combination of low blood pressure, deteriorating renal function and increased plasma potassium could result in arrhythmias and deaths in heart failure patients."

And finally, there are calcium channel blockers. These block electrical transmission in the heart, causing blood pressure to sink. Absurd. Calcium is the chief substance required for igniting and controlling heart health and the strength of contractions for distribution of oxygen and nutrients. Blocking it is like asking for sudden death. If that's not bad enough, this class of medications is also notorious for causing cancer.

In 2013, *The Journal of the American Medical Association* (JAMA) published a study from the Fred Hutchinson Cancer Research Center, theorizing that calcium channel blockers may cause breast cancer. The study monitored more than 1,700 women between the ages of 55 and 74. They were divided into three groups: a control group that was cancer-free and two more groups that included women who had either been diagnosed with invasive lobular cancer or invasive ductal breast cancer. Shockingly, women who were on the meds for a period of 10 years increased their risk of developing lobular and ductal breast cancer by a whopping 2.5 times! [8]

Overall, scientific journals from around the world have shown that people who take blood pressure meds are at a higher risk of dying or being hospitalized for cardiac procedures, regardless of any blood pressure lowering effects from the meds. Researchers from The New York University School of Medicine monitored 44,000 people who were at risk for atherosclerosis (hardening of the arteries). They wrote that the most common, nasty side effects of popular heart medications were "fatigue, headache, upset stomach, weight gain, Type II diabetes."

The research of both past and present continues to show a glaringly obvious truth—that blood pressure meds are the problem, not the solution. Fortunately, there are wildly effective and safe natural medicines available to us. We don't have to resort to risky prescription drugs. All of the available natural cures can help you control your blood pressure, optimize heart health, bust unruly blood clots, and increase the distribution of oxygen and nutrients throughout the body—WITHOUT side effects. But first you'll want to wean off your blood pressure meds. There's a right and a wrong way to it.

How to Safely Wean Off Blood Pressure Meds

If you're currently taking prescription blood pressure drugs, don't stop cold turkey. Wean off them gradually. To begin, take the normal dose of your prescription *every other day* for two weeks, then *every third day* for two more weeks. After four weeks, your body should be completely weaned from the meds and you can safely abstain. During this time, you can safely take the alternatives mentioned below, though you will want to abstain from rauwolfia until fully weaned.

The Natural Alternatives Pharma Doesn't Want You to Know About

For a medicine to be truly effective, it can't be more dangerous than the illness it's trying to treat. Duh. This simple approach to health has been forgotten in favor of massive profits. Gone are the days of "First do no harm." The growing mortality rates from blood pressure meds prove it.

Fortunately, and to the surprise of most, you can ditch all blood pressure drugs and switch to Mother Nature's healthier alternatives—which are very similar molecularly, but very safe!

Natural compounds that treat blood pressure were discovered by the same industry that conceals them. That's because the design of prescription drugs is guided by ethnobotany—the study of plants and their medicinal relationship to humans. When confirmed beneficial by Big Pharma, the active ingredients are plucked from a "natural product lead" and identified in a lab using state-of-the-art chemistry methods.

Once the active, natural compound is characterized, the pharmaceutical industry rearranges a few atoms in hopes of preserving the plant's medicinal qualities in their own, newly-created drug. This allows for patents and monopoly rights to be created, protecting the altered copycat. Unfortunately, once mixed up, the new pharmaceutical creation comes with less efficacy and more side effects. Meanwhile, the safer, cheaper and more effective plant-based predecessor is forgotten, covered up, and simply not taught in med schools.

The story of the malaria drug artemisinin (derived from naturally occurring wormwood) is one of the most compelling examples of the industry's ethos—endless pharmaceutical theft from nature. In 1967, founding father of The People's Republic of China, Mao Zedong, commissioned a secret military project to discover new treatments for malaria.

A mosquito-borne illness caused by microorganisms known as Plasmodia, malaria leads to the destruction of oxygen-carrying red blood cells and ultimately death. A massive threat to Mao's military, Plasmodia developed resistance to chloroquine and other anti-malarial drugs being used at the time. In response, Mao recruited 600 scientists to overcome the scourge. The army of scientists used two chief tactics: ethnobotany and organic chemistry. They discovered sweet wormwood as the definitive cure for malaria.

More recently, by analyzing ancient medical journals and more than 2,000 herbal remedies, chemist Tu Youyou and her team built from Mao's discoveries. They used state-of-the-art chemistry methods to confirm and identify sweet wormwood's antimalarial properties more specifically.

The primary active ingredients were obtained by cold water extraction (tea) and eventually named artemisinin. This "whole herb extract" became one of the most successful treatments in history for malaria! Further studies by Tu used ethyl ether extractions (a chemistry method that isolates single compounds from whole botanical sources) to identify the most potent ingredient. In her Nobel Prize Biography she wrote, "On October 4, 1971, we observed that sample number 191 of the Qinghao (sweet wormwood) ethyl ether extract showed 100% effectiveness in inhibiting malaria parasites in rodent malaria."

In 2015, Tu received the Nobel Prize in Physiology or Medicine for her work. But her discovery of natural wormwood actives was overshadowed by the pharmaceutical mimics of artemisinin, namely dihydroartemisinin (a prescription copy-cat of sweet wormwood), which was positioned as the anti-malaria blockbuster. Even today though, this pharmaceutical, stripped-down version of wormwood is proving worthless in the face of Plasmodia (which has begun building drug resistance) . . . yet sweet wormwood tea remains the true blockbuster, known as far back as when Mao ruled. [10,11,12]

Product Pick

Herb Pharm Wormwood
DOSE: 3-6 mg/lb daily until infection gone
EXAMPLE: 450-900 mg daily for 150 lb person
BEST TIME TO TAKE: Anytime for 5-10 days

This reverse engineering of the elemental secrets of plants isn't new. It's been going on since the first beaker was dropped on the sterile laboratory floor of Big Pharma. Aspirin is a knockoff of white willow bark. Pseudoephedrine was inspired by the use of ma huang for asthma in Chinese medicine. Today's painkillers morphine, codeine, thebaine, and others are the bastard children of the much safer and less addictive poppy plant; and many anticancer drugs come from Madagascar periwinkle and other natural compounds as outlined in *Over-The Counter Natural Cures Expanded.*

The drug industry tries to obfuscate the robbery. They want the public and media to think they intuitively invent blockbuster medications out of thin air, and that drugs are the only option. Thanks to widespread ignorance, this scheme cements the doctor-patient-drug-insurance charade in the minds of patients. It keeps people forever drinking from the pharmaceutical trough, until their deaths.

Natural medicine not only predates civilization—it's older than humanity itself. *The New York Times* reminded us that "many animals self-medicate with plants: In Panama, members of the raccoon family known as coatis rub minty tree resin through their fur to deter fleas, ticks and lice, and some great apes and monkeys swallow mildly toxic leaves seemingly to fight infestations of parasitic worms."

Hairless and still learning to use their opposable thumbs, our ancestors were always on the hunt for plant-based medicines. Modern day science has shown these work better than today's pharmaceuticals.

Between 50 and 70 A.D., the Greek surgeon Dioscorides learned how to make balms, elixirs, and anesthetics from hundreds of plants such as peppermint, hemlock, and cannabis. He published his findings in a pharmacopoeia eventually known as *De Materia Medica,* which has remained the go-to reference for medicinal chemistry for over 1500 years! Since then, clinical science has proven that cannabis oils have anti-cancer, anti-glaucoma, and anti-seizure effects. [13]

This same tedious process of finding new medicines from nature gave rise to three of the most effective natural products for creating total cardiovascular health—hawthorn, cayenne, and rauwolfia. In time though, all three of these were hidden and ultimately forbidden by the pharmaceutical business model, which prefers the stripped-down, costly, and risky synthetic versions (because they can patent those and make big profits). Fortunately, each and every one of these natural cardiovascular cures is readily available.

For moderate hypertension and prevention, hawthorn is usually the first choice. In addition to relaxing arteries to lower blood pressure, it also strengthens the heart and dismembers unruly blood clots on contact, without excessive bleeding. History has shown this repeatedly.

The successful use of hawthorn dates all the way back to the 17th century when it was popularized by French doctor, Henri Leclerc. Today it's a mainstay in Europe and many other parts of the world for total heart health.

The Department of Chemistry at Cork Institute of Technology (CIT) showcased hawthorn's medicinal properties in the medical journal *Pharmacognosy Review*. Commenting on its proven efficacy, they highlighted hawthorn's safety, saying it has no herb-drug interactions and is highly recommended "in treatment strategies surrounding cardiovascular disease, especially in the early stages of disease progression." [14]

Confirming these findings, *The American Journal of Health-System Pharmacy* published that "Hawthorn is a fruit-bearing shrub with a long history as a medicinal substance. Uses have included the treatment of digestive ailments, dyspnea, kidney stones, and cardiovascular disorders. Today, hawthorn is used primarily for various cardiovascular conditions. The cardiovascular effects of hawthorn are believed to be the result of positive inotropic [relaxed heart contractions] activity, ability to increase the integrity of the blood vessel wall and improve coronary blood flow, and positive effects on oxygen utilization."

Decades of research show hawthorn should be used daily as a preventive measure, at the very least, and by anyone suffering form cardiovascular disease. For detailed usage instructions, read my book, *Over-The-Counter Natural Cures Expanded.*

Product Pick

Starwest Botanicals Hawthorn Berry Powder

DOSE: 15 to 20 milligrams per kilogram of body weight two to three times per day.

EXAMPLE: a 150-pound person would take 1000 to 1400 mg twice daily.

BEST TIME TO TAKE: Morning and night, with or without meal.

For more aggressive blood pressure control, hawthorn can be safely combined with cayenne, rauwolfia, or both. All three work in different ways to suppress extreme high blood pressure on the spot.

Consumed for over 6000 years, cayenne peppers contain a family of compounds known as capsaicinoids. It wasn't until the early 2000's that cayenne's true medicinal properties were elucidated. Clinical trials show that healing cayenne actives work both as a topical medicine for pain and orally for cardiovascular and anti-clotting benefits. They're also a great tool for endurance athletes, courtesy of enhancing circulation and oxygen distribution.

To temper the stress put on arteries, whole herb cayenne works as a vasodilator (meaning it widens the blood vessels) and decreases the production of compounds made by the brain that cause high blood pressure. It also works directly on the smooth muscle tissue of coronary arteries to halt or slow the inflammatory process that leads atherosclerosis. Working overtime at protecting the heart, cayenne also inhibits excessive platelet aggregation, which means that—similar to hawthorn—it stops blood clots without causing excessive bleeding.

In 2012 positive evidence for heart-healthy cayenne compounds became so common that the American Chemical Society (ACS) published the cardiovascular findings of Zhen-Yu Chen, PhD, a professor of Food and Nutritional Science at the Chinese University of Hong Kong. "We concluded that capsaicinoids [cayenne actives] were beneficial in improving a range of factors related to heart and blood vessel health." Among them were the inhibition of a gene that produces a compound that forces muscles around blood vessels to constrict—known as cyclooxygenase-2. By blocking it, muscles are better able to relax and widen, allowing for more blood to flow when taking whole herb capsaicin from cayenne.[15]

Most recently, researchers writing for medical journal *Open Heart* published their findings after reviewing the effects of orally administered cayenne to rodents. In a paper titled, "Capsaicin May Have Important Potential For Promoting Vascular and Metabolic Health," they showed that cayenne stimulates endothelial nitric oxide synthase (eNOS) activity, which is vital for opening up arteries and ensuring blood flow during times of exercise and stress. This translated into better artery function, reduction in atherosclerosis (most notably in diabetics) and a decrease in angina. It also slowed progression of non-alcoholic fatty liver disease and curbed thickening of the heart, metabolic syndrome, hypertension, obesity, and gastric ulceration.[16]

One challenge to cayenne supplementation is the discomfort that many people expect from hot peppers such as gastrointestinal (GI) distress and acid reflux. To overcome this, it's best to take a cayenne product that is formulated with the stomach-coating and protecting abilities of marshmallow root. Used for more than 2,000 years, this risk-free root comes as a tea, tincture, or supplement. Producing a cooling type effect, it allows for cayenne use without GI distress, stomach discomfort, or acid reflux.

Product Pick

Wild Harvest Cayenne
DOSE: 10-30 mg/per kg of body weight
EXAMPLE: 700 mg to 2g (1-4 capsules) for 150 lb person
BEST TIME TO TAKE: After a meal

Product Pick

Nature's Sunshine Marshmallow
DOSE: 7-14 mg/per kg of body weight
EXAMPLE: 450 to 1 g (1-2 capsules) for 150 lb person
BEST TIME TO TAKE: Anytime on empty stomach
(1 hour after or before a meal)

And finally, there's rauwolfia. This ancient, Ayurvedic medicine was first written about in Sanskrit as Sarpagandha and Chandra. In the early 16th century, German physician Leonhard Rauwolf studied the plant while traveling in India. The natural medicine was so effective for his patients that it soon became synonymous of the doctor's name.

Later, in the 1950s, rauwolfia's undeniable ability to safely lower blood pressure prompted chemists to study and isolate its active ingredients. A family of alkaloids was identified, and the medicinal extract—reserpine—was believed to be the most pharmacologically active—but today we know it's the synergy of all the alkaloids that lends safety and efficacy. Ciba Pharmaceuticals (now Novartis) began selling the natural extract and the medicine's vast benefits went mainstream. But it was soon lost to newer, more profitable, synthetic versions of the medicine.[17,18]

In 1954, after widespread use, Joseph Monachino wrote about rauwolfia's effectiveness and safety. Writing for *Economic Botany*, he stated that rauwolfia "had recently been admitted in American and European clinical medicine as hypotensive and hypnotic drugs. In addition to lowering blood pressure quite efficiently, apparently without dangerous side-effects, habit formation, withdrawal symptoms or contraindication, these drugs have a sedative or tranquilizing action, said to result from a depressing effect on the hypothalamus."[19]

Unfortunately since then, rauwolfia has been largely forgotten. It started with erroneous statements accusing the natural compound of increasing breast cancer and other illnesses. All were baseless and simply the result of an orchestrated media campaign to get rid of rauwolfia as a safe and effective treatment for dangerously high blood pressure. It worked and ever since, pharmaceutical medications have stolen the limelight.

Big Pharma has essentially rewritten history in favor of patent rights and the monopoly that comes with man-made drugs that trump profits from natural medicines like rauwolfia. Today you won't find a single physician who has even heard of rauwolfia or its health benefits, let alone understands how best to use it. Fortunately for readers, you can get this natural medicine at Amazon.com without a prescription (see product pick).

Using rauwolfia takes a bit of self-experimentation. To start, an average of 100 to 500mg per day of whole herb rauwolfia is suggested for those with extreme, chronic high blood pressure. Splitting the dose to twice per day is most beneficial for anyone who needs the drastic lowering effects. Otherwise, for general use, it can be taken once in the evening to curb high blood pressure and to also encourage sleep. If taking with hawthorn and cayenne, less rauwolfia is more. In other words, 50 to 300mg per day might be sufficient instead of the higher doses mentioned above. Beware: excessive fatigue is a sign of taking too much.

Product Pick

Panchaveda Rauwolfia

DOSE: 2-8 mg/per kg

EXAMPLE: 100 to 500mg for a 150 lb person

BEST TIME TO TAKE: Morning and night, with or without food

In total, rauwolfia, cayenne, and hawthorn have all been forgotten due to the rise in synthetic drugs and the twisted pharmaceutical business model that shuns natural medicine and science in favor of profits.

Yet amazingly, all three forgotten cures are still available for use among those who are privy to their benefits! The switch is as simple as weaning off meds and deciding which product or combo of products is best for you. In a matter of weeks, you'll experience greater energy and weight loss, courtesy of your hormones rebounding.

It's important to note that when making the switch to natural medicine, your blood pressure numbers may not hit the extreme lows that they did while you were on meds. That doesn't mean the natural cures "aren't working"! Artificially low blood pressure numbers are considered drug-induced lows and are not reflective of true health.

Most people forget this and go into a panic as soon as their numbers creep back up to a normal, healthier level, when on natural products. But rest assured, you don't need to adhere to the goal of maintaining blood pressure levels at or near 140/80 (or worse, 115/75)—artificially low numbers that have been pharmaceutically encouraged. When combining all three natural cures—hawthorn, cayenne and rauwolfia—you may be able to lower your blood pressure as needed to match your doctor's goals or the goal of your insurance company, safely and temporarily, but I don't recommend it.

Chapter 1 Bibliography

(1) Szabo, Liz. Millions more American may need high blood pressure medications, study says. *USA Today.* Sept. 11, 2015.

(2) Centers for Disease Control and Prevention. *Poor blood-pressure control puts 5 million older Americans at risk. Focus of new CDC Vital Signs report: how health care systems can help more people take their medicines as directed.* September 13, 2016.

(3) Basso N, Terragno NA. History about the discovery of the renin-angiotensin system. *Hypertension.* 2001 Dec 1;38(6):1246-9.

(4) Cameron JS, Hicks J. Frederick Akbar Mahomed and his role in the description of hypertension at Guy's Hospital. Kidney International. 1996 May;49(5):1488-506.

(5) Brunström, Mattias. Effect of antihypertensive treatment at different blood pressure levels in patients with diabetes mellitus: systematic review and meta-analyses. *British Medical Journal.* 2016; 352.

(6) João Delgado, PhD; Jane A. H. Masoli, MBChB; Kirsty Bowman, MPH; W. David Strain, MD; George A. Kuchel, MD; Kate Walters, PhD; Louise Lafortune, PhD; Carol Brayne, MD; David Melzer, PhD; Alessandro Ble. Outcomes of Treated Hypertension at Age 80 and Older Cohort Analysis of 79,376 Individuals. *Journal of the American Geriatrics Society.* 2017;65(5):995-1003.

(7) Kolata, Gina. Hypertension Guidelines Can Be Eased, Panel Says. *New York Times.* December 18, 2013.

(8) Li CI, Daling JR, Tang MC, Haugen KL, Porter PL, Malone KE. Use of Antihypertensive Medications and Breast Cancer Risk Among Women Aged 55 to 74 Years. *Journal of the American Medical Association Intern Medicine.* 2013;173(17):1629-1637.

(9) Tu Y. Artemisinin-A Gift from Traditional Chinese Medicine to the World (Nobel Lecture). Angewandte Chem Int Ed Engl. 2016 Aug 22;55(35).

(10) Rasoanaivo P, Wright CW, Willcox ML, Gilbert B. Whole plant extracts versus single compounds for the treatment of malaria: synergy and positive interactions. *Malaria Journal.* 2011;10 (Suppl 1):S4.

(11) Cojean S, Hubert V, Le Bras J, Durand R. Resistance
to Dihydroartemisinin. *Emerging Infectious Diseases.*
2006;12(11):1798-1799. doi:10.3201/eid1211.060903.

(12) Nguyen Thi Kim Tuyen, Nguyen Thanh Tong, Nguyen Thuy Nha
Ca, Le Thanh Dong, Huynh Hong Quang, Jeremy Farrar, Guy
Thwaites, Nicholas J. White, Marcel Wolbers and Tran Tinh Hien.
Rapid decline in the susceptibility of Plasmodium falciparum to
dihydroartemisinin–piperaquine in the south of Vietnam. *Malaria
Journal.* 201716:27.

(13) Dioscorides Pedanius, Tess Anne Osbaldeston, and Robert P. Wood.
De Materia Medica: Being an Herbal with Many Other Medicinal
Materials: Written in Greek in the First Century of the Common
Era: a New Indexed Version in Modern English.

(14) Tassell MC, Kingston R, Gilroy D, Lehane M, Furey A. Hawthorn
in the treatment of cardiovascular disease. *Pharmacognosy Reviews.*
2010;4(7):32-41.

(15) American Chemical Society (ACS). "Hot pepper compound could
help hearts." ScienceDaily. ScienceDaily, 27 March 2012

(16) McCarty MF, DiNicolantonio JJ, O'Keefe JH Capsaicin may have
important potential for promoting vascular and metabolic health
Open Heart 2015;2:e000262.

(17) Vakil, Gal Rustom. A Clinical Trial of Rauwolfia Serpentina in
Essential Hypertension. From the Cardiological Department, King
Edward Memorial Hospital, Bombay, India Received January 4,
1949.

(18) Plummer, A.J., Earl, A., Schneider, J.A., Trapold, J. and Barrett, W.
(1954), PHARMACOLOGY OF *RAUWOLFIA* ALKALOIDS,
INCLUDING RESERPINE. Annals of the New York Academy of
Sciences, 59: 8–21.

(19) Monachino, Joseph. Rauvolfia serpentina—Its history, botany and
medical use. *Economic Botany.* October 1954, Volume 8, Issue 4,
pp 349–365.

CHAPTER TWO

2

"High Cholesterol" Is a Fake Disease

Cholesterol is a versatile compound that is vital to the functioning of the human body. Just like everything else, cholesterol levels differ greatly among individuals.

Some things will never change. I'll always be a bald, tattoo-sporting chemist who sings rap music too loud while driving my kids to school. My kids will always know more than most adults about the benefits of individualism over collectivism. And most people will blindly try to lower their cholesterol with Lipitor (or other cholesterol-lowering drugs) to save them from heart attack and stroke.

High cholesterol is a fake disease. It was invented so that drug companies could sell you cholesterol-lowering drugs (statins). The myth of "high cholesterol" is so prevalent that The American Academy of Pediatrics and The American Heart Association issued guidelines allowing children as young as 8 years old to be placed on cholesterol-lowering drugs. Yet there isn't a single study to support the claim that high cholesterol is even dangerous. Considering the many side effects of statins, childhood mortality rates are poised to go through the roof!

This shit needs to end now.

Brace yourself. I'm going to spoon-feed you the REAL facts about heart disease and the drugs being falsely prescribed to thwart it. I promise these facts will taste better than the bullshit sandwich your doctor has been feeding you and your kids.

I'm all for living young. I study medicine like most guys study Harley-Davidsons. I've mastered natural medicine so that I can have more time to love my family, drink wine, talk shit, and watch the sunset while my kids argue and fight in the pool. I know for certain that if I had to choose between having sex with a carny or letting my kids choke down Lipitor for the rest of their lives, I'd be begging for a Trojan.

In my book, *Over-The-Counter Natural Cures Expanded*, I exposed the overt dangers of Lipitor and many other popular statin drugs. I also put a spotlight on the science that proves how natural medicine, costing less than 10 bucks per month, trumps them all! Readers were dismayed to learn about the insidious business model that sold Lipitor and similar meds without any proof of preventing heart attack or stroke. Meanwhile, statins create horrific side effects like rhabdomyolysis (muscle breakdown), liver disease, low testosterone, cancer, Parkinson's disease, and more.

In response to the growing awareness of statin dangers, the drug industry is devising a new class of cholesterol-lowering drugs. They're known as PCSK9 inhibitors (code for "Pack up your shit and leave, cause this will fuck you up 9 ways to China"). PCSK9 inhibitors work by shutting down the formation of LDL cholesterol in your body. More risky than their predecessor, these meds drop cholesterol levels to life-threatening lows. Described as going "subterranean," cholesterol bottoms out. You might as well be dead at that point. Toxic and foreign to the body, this insanely low cholesterol level prompts the immune system to fight back with a plethora of antibodies that attack the drug—and sadly, the body—while leaving patients with a host of auto-immune disorders.

The Art of Turning Healthy People into Patients

Choosing sexy-time with a carny inside of a smoky, beat-up RV as an alternative to taking cholesterol-lowering meds might seem a bit extreme to some. But the system is designed to create this status quo and make people think toxic meds are OK. The uninformed are easy to fool.

Think about it. When was the last time you were taught anything substantial about medicine? Instead you're bombarded with drug commercials consisting of 15 seconds of benefits, followed by 45 seconds of side effects.

This lack of education helps the industry swindle your uninformed ass into taking drugs. If you can look beyond the Kardashians and political antics for a few minutes, you'll see this corporate business model in plain sight. It makes you fear an unknown or misunderstood enemy and offers a false, albeit profitable, solution.

According to the American Heart Association (AHA) (another arm of the pharmaceutical industry), over 105 million Americans have total cholesterol levels of 200 mg/dL or higher. To the pharmaceutical industry, this equates to 105 million potential customers. In order to turn these millions of people into patients, America has been told this cholesterol level is bad for them—so the lower the better. (You were probably also incorrectly taught that eating too many egg yolks is bad for you, because eggs yolks contain cholesterol. When in reality, egg yolks are one of the healthiest foods you can eat.) [1]

Rising cholesterol is not a disease—it's simply an observation of biology. Imagine how ridiculous it would be to say that "Most people with heart disease have a refrigerator; therefore, a fridge is the cause of it." High cholesterol is no different. In other words it's a fact of life, not a sign of illness.

With dollar signs in their eyes, drug companies have launched a massive fear campaign to warn people about cholesterol. Being led by the pharmaceutically-compliant National Cholesterol Education Program (NCEP), the campaign convinced nearly the entire world via the media that LDL cholesterol is bad and that total cholesterol levels should remain below 200 mg/dL in order to prevent heart disease. (Of the nine nerdy members of the NCEP, eight had financial ties to cholesterol-lowering drug makers like Pfizer, Merck, Bristol-Myers Squibb, and AstraZeneca. This fact was concealed when the NCEP made its recommendations public.)

The professional alarmists of the NCEP successfully created a "cholesterol problem" in the minds of millions. Meanwhile, they provided a false solution: cholesterol-lowering drugs. This scheme worked, because prior to the scary advertising disguised as education, nobody even knew what the hell cholesterol was. Hundreds of millions of people had no idea they were even "sick". . . think about that!

As a young kid, I had a hunch that most people were stupid, including some of my high school teachers. (Maybe that's why I skipped school so often.)

I was wrong. People are fuckin' *incredibly* stupid.

The so-called disease of "high cholesterol" causes no fever, no coughing, no labored breathing, no heart palpitations, no hormone imbalance, no pain, no nothing! How do you convince someone who doesn't feel sick that they're suffering from a terminal illness like "hypercholesterolemia"—a term invented to describe high cholesterol—and subsequently get them to take meds, every day, for life? Through ignorance, that's how.

I've done some stupid things throughout my life. I rafted the Pacuare River in Costa Rica during a flood. As we busted through muddy swaths of man-eating waves, boulders smashed into each other and echoed beneath our raft on the river bottom as the rogue current pushed them downstream. Another time, while traveling through Mexico, I pierced my nipples to see what it would feel like (I was sober). As a hostile teen, I even got caught up in a high-speed police chase, which ended with a loaded gun being pressed to my temple.

Even after all of that, I'm proud to say I've never been scammed by the cholesterol-lowering drug rip-off. I've always known it's nothing more than a home run heist for Wall Street.

Pfizer's blockbuster drug Lipitor became the first prescription drug to make more than $10 billion in annual sales. In 2017, Forbes Magazine showed statins are earning drug pushers $26 billion in annual sales—that's greater than the combined GDP of more than *half* the nations on Earth! Outrageous.

Do you think that's enough money to take over medical journals with ghostwriting, ads, and lobbying? Pharma has profited so hugely, they can push the cholesterol-lowering agenda even further by instilling as much fear into the public as they want.

Before you get victimized by this scam, ask your doctor the following intelligent questions (expect them to look at you in shock):

Question #1. Explain to me why EVERYONE should have the same exact cholesterol level?

This is a legit question. Stating that everyone should have the same cholesterol levels is like asserting that all women should have the same sized breasts and all men should have the same sized package. (Wait, scratch that. Bad analogy.) Should all people have the same shoe size?—and if they don't, it means their foot needs surgery?!

This is stupid thinking. If your doctor insists that we should all have cholesterol levels below 200 mg/dL, then ask him or her:

Question #2. What are some studies I could read to learn more about high cholesterol being dangerous?

Your doctor may go into a well-crafted sales pitch about how high cholesterol is responsible for plaque build-up among the arteries of the heart. But that's ridiculous because cholesterol is found everywhere in the body. This means so-called "high" levels would be blocking off all regions, not just those of your heart.

Cadaver studies show that 90% of the time, blockage only occurs within the coronary arteries, not among other parts like legs, arms, fingers, or anywhere else. So by definition, cholesterol can't be the cause of blockage—because cholesterol is everywhere in the body. It does not cause plaque everywhere when it rises. (If it did, then there would be plaque everywhere in your body.)

Plus, *Time Magazine* highlighted the science showing that "most heart attack victims have LOW cholesterol." This just confirmed the findings of scientists at The University of California Los Angeles who announce, "A new national study has shown that nearly 75 percent of patients hospitalized for a heart attack had [low] cholesterol levels that would indicate they were not at high risk for a cardiovascular event, based on current national cholesterol guidelines." Therefore, if high cholesterol actually caused plaque, then why the hell do most heart attack victims have low cholesterol levels? [2]

Fact is, there are no studies proving that high cholesterol causes plaque. Not one. Cholesterol is very important for the body, and levels over 200 mg/dL will never kill you. Just the opposite, research shows that higher cholesterol is healthy as you age! There are plenty of studies to prove that! If you remember only one thing from this chapter, it should be *the higher your cholesterol, the longer you live.*

5 Facts About Cholesterol Your Doctor Doesn't Know

Cholesterol is a versatile compound that is vital to the functioning of the human body. Just like everything else, cholesterol levels differ greatly among individuals. In humans, cholesterol serves five main functions:

1. Cholesterol is used by the body to manufacture steroids, or cortisone-like hormones, including the sex hormones. These hormones include testosterone, estrogen, and cortisone. Combined, these hormones control a myriad of bodily functions.

2. Cholesterol helps the liver produce bile acids. These acids are essential for proper digestion of fats and in ridding the body of waste products.

3. Cholesterol acts to interlock "lipid molecules," which stabilize cell membranes. Like pieces of a puzzle, cholesterol is the building block for all bodily tissues.

4. Cholesterol is an essential part of the myelin sheath. Similar to the coating on copper wire, the myelin sheath ensures that the brain functions properly by aiding the passage of electrical impulses. Without the myelin sheath, it becomes difficult to focus and we can lose memory. This is why people on cholesterol-lowering drugs are notorious for having bad memory. Few users recognize this side effect because they forgot how important having a memory was.

5. Cholesterol has beneficial effects on the immune system. Men with high cholesterol have stronger immune systems than those with low cholesterol. This is proven by them having more strains of probiotics and assassin-like cells from the immune system that fend off foreign invaders.

As you can see, cholesterol is pretty fucking beneficial. Without enough of it, you're screwed. Artificially lowering your cholesterol with drugs is a death wish. Due to its vast importance, cholesterol must be circulated to all parts of the body via the estimated 100,000 miles of arteries and veins within the adult human body. To understand how cholesterol circulates through the body, recall the fact that oil and water do not mix. Cholesterol is an oily substance (termed a lipid) and cannot blend smoothly with water-based blood. In order to transport this non-water soluble lipid through the bloodstream, the body packages cholesterol into special "vehicles" called lipoproteins.

The Truth About HDL and LDL Cholesterol

The main cholesterol-carrying vehicle in the body is termed low-density lipoprotein or LDL. Because LDL carries the lipid known as cholesterol, it's referred to as LDL cholesterol. (Technically, LDL cholesterol and HDL cholesterol aren't even true cholesterol molecules—which makes the theory of "bad cholesterol" even more ludicrous. It's just empty sales rhetoric designed to instill fear in the public.)

Another form of lipoprotein (and there are many) is high-density lipoprotein or HDL cholesterol. The notion that one form of cholesterol is "bad" and the other is "good" is as real as the Easter Bunny. This commonly mistaken notion is based on the fact that LDL cholesterol has been found to be one of many components of arterial plaque, along with saturated fat, calcium, and cholesterol. Meanwhile, HDL has been shown to transport cholesterol back to the liver. That's it.

Whether a person's cholesterol is high or low, LDL cholesterol will still become a component of plaque. Plaque is simply a necessity of life. The body is programmed to save itself by using cholesterol of all kinds, regardless of their levels. Therefore, no relation to the amount of LDL cholesterol in the blood and the severity of plaque exists, whatsoever.

Plaque is nature's "Band Aid" to the damaged inner layer of the artery, known medically as the endothelium. Without the packaging of LDL cholesterol, we would not be alive. How can LDL cholesterol be bad? It's like saying the immune system is harmful to us because it attacks biological nasties in our body.

Having grasped what cholesterol really is, we can now move on to understanding its relationship to heart disease (i.e., atherosclerosis). Once you learn the basics of how heart disease develops, you can make informed actions to protect yourself. (And no, this does NOT require lowering your cholesterol!)

What Really Causes Heart Disease?

Atherosclerosis is the hardening and narrowing of the arteries. It's an inflammatory response initiated by damage to the endothelium. The endothelium is the innermost layer of the arteries. Damage to the endothelium can happen anywhere in the body, but 90% of the time it happens in the spaghetti-sized arteries of the heart (coronary arteries), probably due to the mechanical stress in this region.

If you want to preserve your heart health, don't bother trying to artificially lower your LDL cholesterol levels. It's far more important to prevent damage to the endothelium of the arteries. Many biological disturbances, including poor lifestyle habits, can damage the inner layer of the coronary artery.

10 Reasons Why You Might Have Heart Disease:

- Oxidative stress

- Infection

- Smoking

- High blood sugar and insulin attributed to insulin resistance

- Type II diabetes (Beat it in 30 days by reading Over-The-Counter Natural Cures Expanded)

- Increased levels of homocysteine attributed to lack of folate and nutritive B vitamins (best source of these vitamins are Brewer's Yeast and whole eggs)

- Increased levels of cortisol (i.e. stress)

- Lack of exercise (Use www.18minworkout.com)

- Lack of nutritive vitamin C (best source is citrus fruits)

To protect your heart, work on eliminating all of the above "inflammatory disturbances" from your life. By doing so, you'll prevent plaque build-up and the subsequent atherosclerosis or premature death that may follow.

Once damage occurs to the inner layer (endothelium) of the coronary artery, the body's natural repair mechanism takes over. This is because as humans, we're equipped with a natural instinct to live. The repair mechanism begins by circulating levels of low density lipoproteins (LDLs) into the damaged area, particularly between the smooth muscle layer and endothelium of the artery. Once LDLs move into the damaged area of the endothelium, an alteration in endothelium function takes place. This alteration begins the inflammation cascade.

To signal for help, the endothelium begins producing reactive oxygen species (ROS). Like a citizen calling 911, this attracts the immune cells to the damaged site, which forms a protective shield around the damaged area of the blood vessel. Eventually, the combination of LDL, immune cells, muscle cells, and debris from the initial damage create "plaque."

The most important thing to understand is that plaque is nature's fix to damage within the arterial wall. Plaque forms in response to this damage, regardless of LDL cholesterol levels. This, in part, explains why researchers have failed to find a correlation between levels of cholesterol and the growth of atherosclerosis.

If damage to the endothelium persists, atherosclerotic plaque accumulates on the arterial walls. This leads to decreased blood flow from the heart, which prevents oxygen and nutrients from being disseminated throughout the body. It's similar to a grocery store suddenly dead-bolting its doors shut, preventing access to the food inside. A chronic lack of oxygen and nutrients leads to major problems not only for your heart, but also for your brain, lungs, kidneys, penile reaction, and eventually every bodily system.

Over time, build-up of atherosclerotic plaque initiates heart attack and stroke. Sometimes this happens without warning. As the artery narrows, tiny blood clots (which are normally harmless) become a death threat. In normal circumstances, these tiny blood clots are usually capable of passing through a healthy artery—but when the artery is narrowed, they get caught in the plaque and prevent blood flow. If an artery is blocked in the heart, a heart attack is the result. If a blockage occurs in the brain, a stroke is the result. Quitting sugar and supplementing with folate-rich Brewer's Yeast and nattokinase (as taught in next chapter) can delay and stop the premature progression of plaque.

Product Pick

BlueBonnet Unfortified Brewers Yeast
DOSE: 1-2 tablespoons in water per 150 lbs
BEST TIME TO TAKE: Morning and night (with food)

High Cholesterol Increases Longevity

Most people can agree that cholesterol-lowering drugs are bad for human health. But people seem to have a tough time grasping the fact that high cholesterol actually INCREASES lifespan. All you need to do is look at large populations of humans and measure their cholesterol levels and longevity, and the truth becomes clear: there is no such thing as "the disease of high cholesterol." Trying to lower cholesterol with medications to below whatever the status quo number might be for that given year, is suicide. There are plenty of studies from around the world to prove this.

Researchers at the University of San Diego called attention to epidemiological studies showing that high cholesterol in people over 75 years of age is protective, rather than harmful. Reported by *BBC News,* Professor Beatriz Rodriquez of the University of Hawaii in Honolulu and colleagues found that men over age 70 who had cholesterol levels between 200 to 219 milligrams per deciliter (mg/dL) were less likely to develop heart disease than those with low cholesterol levels. Elderly men with cholesterol levels of below 160 mg/dL had a 55% greater risk of heart disease.[3]

Other researchers have arrived at similar conclusions. *The European Heart Journal* published the results of a three-year study involving 11,500 patients. Researcher Behar and associates found that in the low cholesterol group (total cholesterol below 160 mg/dL), the relative risk of death was 2.27 times higher compared to those with higher cholesterol. The most common cause of death in the low cholesterol group was cancer, with liver disease being second. Behar's study also linked low blood cholesterol levels less than 160 mg/dL to a twofold-increased risk of death from cancer of the liver, pancreas, and organs that form red blood cells.[4]

These same researchers showed that healthy men without any history of cardiovascular, gastrointestinal, or liver disease—who lower their total cholesterol—have an increased risk of prostate cancer, intracranial hemorrhage, respiratory, kidney, and digestive disease.

The most widely respected medical journal, *The Journal of the American Medical Association,* published a study entitled: "Cholesterol and Mortality. 30 Years of Follow-up from the Framingham Study." Shocking to most readers, this in-depth study showed that after the age of 50, there is no increased overall death rate associated with high cholesterol! There was, however, a direct association between low levels (or dropping levels) of cholesterol and increased death.[5]

Medical researchers reported that cardiovascular death rates increased by 14% for every 1 mg/dL drop in total cholesterol levels per year! That means that every incremental decline in cholesterol led to a corresponding drop in longevity.

Here's the ugly truth: the lower your cholesterol is, the more fucked up your body and health become. (Doesn't that make you want to slam the nearest cholesterol-lowering drug down your throat?!)

For those who have already suffered from heart failure, lowering cholesterol only exacerbates the problem . . . like pouring gasoline over a fire. It'd be better to let your cholesterol rise to naturally higher levels. The *Journal of Cardiac Failure* published the findings of Horwich and colleagues in a paper, "Low Serum Total Cholesterol is Associated with Marked Increase in Mortality in Advanced Heart Failure." In their analysis of 1,134 patients with heart disease, they found that low cholesterol was associated with worse outcomes in heart failure patients and impaired survival, while high cholesterol improved survival rates. Interesting to note, their findings also showed that elevated cholesterol among patients was not associated with hypertension, diabetes, or coronary heart disease.[6]

Low cholesterol has also been linked to depression and anxiety. Dr. Edward Suarez of Duke University found that women with low cholesterol levels (below 160 mg/dL) were more likely to show signs of depression and anxiety relative to women with normal or high cholesterol levels. In 2003 Duke University showed a 20% absolute increase in depression among those taking cholesterol-lowering drugs known as statins. Their results add to the literature linking cholesterol and mood.[7]

The Scandinavian Journal of Primary Health Care published the results of a study looking at cholesterol levels and death among 100,000 patients over the age of 50 years old. Their evidence showed the exact opposite of what Big Pharma insists. Reporting the raw data, the scientists wrote, "For the groups with the highest total cholesterol level, the mortality becomes significantly lower in the oldest age group compared with the group with the lowest total cholesterol." They echoed what many researchers before them found: "These associations indicate that high lipoprotein levels [cholesterol] do not seem to be definitely harmful in the general population."[8]

If you think lowering your total cholesterol level will protect you from heart disease, you may want to seriously rethink your strategy. Lowering cholesterol, whether by prescription drugs or dietary supplements like red yeast rice, has proven to be dangerous and goes against centuries of scientific research findings. High cholesterol is protective rather than detrimental.

How Medical Doctors are Fooled—Selective Citation

Given the wide range of research showing that higher cholesterol is healthy as we age, this begs the question: how does someone successfully convince the entire United States population that each and every person should have the same cholesterol level? Why is there such widespread acceptance of the cholesterol myth?

The belief that low cholesterol prevents heart disease is the result of selective citation rather than scientific results. Selective citation is the art of conveniently citing supportive studies while burying the unsupportive ones.

In addition to smothering unsupportive studies from our medical history, pharmaceutical companies who sell cholesterol-lowering drugs produce brochures, web pages, and various other publications to broadcast the cholesterol-lowering myth to millions. As pointed out by the previous editor of the *New England Journal of Medicine*, Jerome P. Kassirer, MD, major publications such as *Lipid Letter*, *Lipids Online*, and *Lipid Management* are supported and funded by cholesterol-lowering drug makers.

Reaching millions of medical doctors, these publications relentlessly warn of the false dangers of high cholesterol in an attempt to nudge doctors into prescribing cholesterol-lowering drugs. This not only ensures that drug companies profit—it also promotes the cholesterol-lowering myth. Preferential citation, combined with paid publications aimed at medical doctors, guarantees that the pharmaceutical industry can "invent diseases" out of thin air, while also providing the so-called remedy.

Remember, cholesterol is one of the most important molecules in the human body, especially for children whose bodies are still developing. Its respective high and low levels do not cause heart disease or prevent heart attack and stroke (except for people over 70—where higher cholesterol is shown to be protective). To truly live young and disease-free, get your weight in check and adhere to the principles of "nutrient logic" outlined in *Over-The-Counter*

Natural Cures Expanded. You'll not only preserve health, but also wealth, allowing you to live long enough to achieve your dreams and do things you never thought possible. Living young starts with saying "No" to the cholesterol-lowering drug, Lipitor, and all others!

Often when a doctor tries to push Lipitor on a patient, it won't be long before they also try to seduce that patient into taking aspirin. You'll want to ditch that drug, as well. As you'll learn in the next chapter, aspirin slowly destroys the body from the inside out.

Chapter 2 Bibliography

(1) Go AS, Mozaffarian D, Roger VL, Benjamin EJ, Berry JD, Borden
WB, Bravata DM, Dai S, Ford ES, Fox CS, Franco S, Fullerton HJ,
Gillespie C, Hailpern SM, Heit JA, Howard VJ, Huffman MD, Kissela
BM, Kittner SJ, Lackland DT, Lichtman JH, Lisabeth LD, Magid D,
Marcus GM, Marelli A, Matchar DB, McGuire DK, Mohler ER, Moy
CS, Mussolino ME, Nichol G, Paynter NP, Schreiner PJ, Sorlie PD,
Stein J, Turan TN, Virani SS, Wong ND, Woo D, Turner MB; on
behalf of the American Heart Association Statistics Committee and
Stroke Statistics Subcommittee. Heart disease and stroke statistics—
2013 update: a report from the American Heart Association.
Circulation. 2013;127:e6-e245.

(2) Champeau, Rachel. Most heart attack patients' cholesterol levels did
not indicate cardiac risk. UCLA News Room. January 12, 2009.

(3) Hoffman, Bill. Latest Cholesterol Study Finds New Level of Health.
The New York Post. March 5, 2001.

(4) S. Behar, E. Graff, H. Reicher-Reiss, V. Boyko, M. Benderly, A.
Shotan and D. Brunner for the Bezafibrate Infarction Prevention
(BIP) Study Group. Low total cholesterol is associated with high
total mortality in patients with coronary heart disease. *European
Heart Journal* (1997) 18, 52-59.

(5) Anderson KM, Castelli WP, Levy D. Cholesterol and Mortality30
Years of Follow-up From the Framingham Study. *Journal of the
American Medical Association.* 1987;257(16):2176–2180.

(6) Low serum total cholesterol is associated with marked increase in
mortality in advanced heart failure Horwich, Tamara B. et al. Journal
of Cardiac Failure, Volume 8 , Issue 4 , 216–22.

(7) Low Cholesterol Linked to Depression. BBC Online Network,
May 25,1999. T. Partonen, J. Haukka, J. Virtamo, P. R. Taylor, J.
Lönnqvist Association of low serum total cholesterol with major
depression and suicide. British Journal of Psychiatry. 1999 Sep; 175:
259–262.

(8) Bathum L, Depont Christensen R, Engers Pedersen L, Lyngsie Pedersen P, Larsen J, Nexøe J. Association of lipoprotein levels with mortality in subjects aged 50 + without previous diabetes or cardiovascular disease: A population-based register study. *Scandinavian Journal of Primary Health Care.* 2013;31(3):172-180.

3

The Hidden Truth about Aspirin and its Natural Alternative

In a comparison of aspirin and nattokinase, it was found that nature's alternative prevented and reduced the occlusion better and far safer than the over-the-counter blood thinner!

Today most people think of aspirin as a harmless wonder drug that can stop pain, fever, and even prevent heart attack and stroke without risk. Not true. History proves aspirin is ineffective and dangerous.

Thousands of years ago, humans observed injured bears (not the Chicago Bears) gnawing on the bark of white willow trees. Some dude—probably an earlier rendition of The People's Chemist assumed the bears were doing it to relieve pain.

After a long night of drinking away his frustrations with people who talk more than they think, he decided to test his theory. Hungover, the young chemist made a tea from the bark. It tasted like shit. But almost instantly, his discomfort melted away.

Despite his gluttonous indulgence, the crushing pressure on his head was gone. He suffered no side effects, didn't have to pay for anything, and didn't have to grovel for a doctor's prescription. It was like he'd struck the natural medicine lottery. White willow bark became the official pain reliever not only for bears, but also for many other human party-goers astute enough to follow his lead.

Greek physician Hippocrates heard about white willow bark. (He's the same guy whom nerdy nutritionists today quote ad nauseum as saying, "Let food be your medicine and medicine be your food.") Well, thank God Hippocrates started taking tips from chemists. Medicine is more interesting and a lot more fucking reliable than eating an apple a day . . . and definitely more exciting at parties, if that's what you're into.

Eventually, the doctor put the real medicine to use and it worked. White willow bark became the natural drug of choice for pain relief. (It's rumored that Hippocrates later said, "Chemists are awesome tutors and fun to party with.")

As time passed, Big Pharma heard about white willow bark and got excited about profiting off this painkiller. This laid the groundwork for the eventual isolation and synthesis of a molecule known as salicylic acid (SA)—one of many ingredients found in white willow bark and believed to be the primary pain reliever.

To their distress, the pharmaceutical industry couldn't patent the product and therefore couldn't market the natural ingredient as their own. (You can't patent Mother Nature . . . yet.) In order to have a monopoly, they had to alter SA so that it didn't resemble the original form. Carl R. Gerhardt, a chemist, was the first to do so in 1853.

Starting with the parent compound from white willow bark, Gerhardt performed a series of laboratory reactions that created newly formed derivatives of nature. Then he tested them for pain-relieving abilities. His actions yielded a molecular cousin, a fake, a knockoff named acetyl-salicylic acid (ASA). The newly devised "willow bark-wannabe" marked one of the earliest and most profitable thefts from Mother Nature.

Bayer trademarked this knockoff as "Aspirin" in 1889. Some say the name was derived from St. Aspirinius, a Neapolitan bishop who was the patron saint against headaches.

As aspirin grew in popularity, its inherent risks also began surfacing. (So much for being a saint . . .) The small molecular change brought with it big dangers. Like deflating a tire, aspirin depletes the body of life-saving nutrients: folate, iron, potassium, sodium, and vitamin C.

Symptoms associated with aspirin-induced nutrient depletion include: anemia, birth defects, heart disease, elevated homocysteine (a risk factor for heart disease), headache, depression, fatigue, hair loss, insomnia, diarrhea, shortness of breath, pale skin, and suppression of the immune system.[1]

Internal bleeding is one of the biggest risks. Studies show that aspirin users die sooner compared to non-users from the hemorrhaging. This cancels out any perceived or wished-for benefits in the reduction of heart disease or cancer—so-called benefits that are often hyped by Big Pharma.

Aspirin is a class of drugs known as nonsteroidal anti-inflammatory drugs (NSAIDs). Each year, a grossly underestimated 7,600 deaths and 76,000 hospitalizations occur in the United States from the use of aspirin and other NSAIDs like Motrin, Aleve, and Celebrex. Unfortunately, the FDA states that only about 10% of deaths caused by NSAIDs are reported, so the real mortality count is massively larger. The media is either oblivious to this or refuses to acknowledge the elephant in the room.[2]

The same is true with doctors—they just turn the other way and ignore the damage being done. Death caused by any NSAID is usually falsely attributed to the victim being either too damn sick or too damn old. This makes it easy for the medical industry to conceal the side effects and overdoses of aspirin. Meanwhile, aspirin has been pushed onto everyone via massive marketing scams.

Today the average person has been trained to pop an aspirin at the first sign of pain. Who's behind this push? Look no further than Bayer and the U.S. government. This incestuous relationship was spawned before anyone of us were even born. A look through the history books blows the lid off it.

In February 1917 the drug company Bayer lost its American patent on aspirin. They were poised to lose beaucoup-bucks. The profit floodgates were opened up for other companies to make money from selling the chalky white pills.

Bayer wasn't going down without a fight.

Partnering with the U.S. military in 1918, Bayer ensured that troops were intentionally diagnosed with the flu. Even the smallest anomaly in health—fatigue, high temperature, sore throat, dehydration or viral infection—brought an official flu diagnosis to an estimated 50 million people. Reacting to these fake diagnoses, the pharmaceutically compliant media reported that the globe was in the midst of "quite possibly the deadliest plague known to mankind." Enter mass panic and chaos. The need for aspirin was successfully spawned. Enter Bayer.

Positioned as the benevolent savior, Bayer conveniently had stockpiles of aspirin standing by. Always beholden to Pharma, the surgeon general and the U.S. Navy recommended Americans "take Aspirin to treat their flu symptoms." Beaucoup tax money was siphoned from the economy like a broken spring to pay for the military use of aspirin. Bayer and government officials who were financially connected to the money became rich beneficiaries.

(This siphoning of money from government to Big Pharma happens quite regularly, courtesy of artificially created "pandemics." This is a recurring theme throughout history and even today, as you'll soon see with vaccine promotions.)

Fast forward to present time—Dr. Karen M. Starko has written about the deadly effects of aspirin. Her writings suggest that during the 1918 "calamity," aspirin probably did more harm than good. More specifically, aspirin—NOT the flu—is most likely what killed many of the people who took it during the so-called "historical flu outbreak!" In the mad rush to protect corporate and government profits, people's lives were lost while Bayer's profits enriched.[3]

But in 1918 the American population was in the grips of mass delusion and had no idea that the cure was killing them. Aspirin was considered their "wonder drug." Bayer launched an aggressive advertising campaign, spoon-feeding Americans lie after lie about how "pure" their newly, un-patented aspirin was. (Never mind that even back then, a first year chemistry student could yield pure aspirin in the lab.)

Meanwhile, the so-called "flu epidemic" was reaching its peak. People fell for the lies and gobbled up aspirin like it was Cheerios. After many of them died, their deaths were conveniently blamed on the flu.

Playing their role in spreading mass delusion, the always pharmaceutically compliant *Journal of the American Medical Association* suggested people swallow 1,000 milligrams of aspirin every three hours to treat the flu! Do the math—that's like taking 25 standard 325-milligram aspirin tablets in a 24-hour period. It was a money-making heyday for Bayer and a curse for patients. Not much has changed since 1918.

In 1986 Dr. Otis R. Bowen, the Secretary of Health and Human Services, issued a warning reminding parents that children and teenagers with flu symptoms "should not be given aspirin." When used for the flu or chicken pox, aspirin puts users at risk for Reye's syndrome, a disorder that causes organs to shut down and large amounts of bloody, watery liquid to accumulate in the lungs.[4]

In time, pharmacologist John Vane discovered the deadly actions of aspirin. On the one hand, he found that it blocks the production of an enzyme known as COX (cyclooxygenase). Downstream this prevents inflammation, swelling, pain, and fever. But on the other hand, it creates a risky trade-off. In addition to being a COX inhibitor, aspirin also stifles the formation of healing compounds made by the body. Crucial for physiological support, these compounds protect the stomach from damage by hydrochloric acid, maintain kidney function, and stop internal bleeding. Once the body is exposed to the deadly blood thinner, ulcers, kidney failure, and internal bleeding ensue. Vane won the Nobel Prize for his work and somehow the media is silent on his warning.

Bayer wasn't the slightest bit concerned about these award-winning findings. Like doctors, they simply ignored the Nobel Prize-winning science. Expanding their market reach, they pushed "baby" aspirin (i.e., low dose aspirin) to protect against heart attack, stroke, and cancer. But the infantile dose proved just as harmful as the regular dose.

Writing for *The New York Times,* Dr. Neena S. Abraham said, "If your physician has suggested you take aspirin to reduce your risk of heart disease, it is important to remember that even small doses of daily aspirin—including 'baby aspirin,' at a dose of 81 milligrams daily—can increase your risk of ulcers and bleeding." Buffered or enteric-coated aspirin won't protect you, either.

Judith P. Kelly of the Slone Epidemiology Unit at the Boston University School of Medicine warned that "all forms of aspirin carry risk." Protective covering or not, the white pill still paralyzes the production of physiologically-important compounds in our body.

The natural predecessor, white willow bark tea, remains the safer option for pain relief. Even if you're "allergic" to aspirin, the tea is a fantastic alternative for pain relief or even high fevers, as it doesn't contain the problematic ASA (acetyl-salicylic-acid) that spurs most allergic reactions.

Due to the drug's inherent risks, it's best to ignore aspirin for cardiovascular health. In other words, you're not going to protect your heart by taking aspirin. Fortunately, unruly blood clots that lead to heart attack and stroke are best curbed using hawthorn and cayenne (as outlined in *Over-The-Counter Natural Cures Expanded*). For those who have been diagnosed with heart disease, or who are looking for total cardiovascular health, nattokinase is among the safest and most effective aspirin alternatives.

Product Pick

Frontier Co-Op Certified Organic White Willow Bark Tea
DOSE: Steep 1-5 tablespoons in water as needed for pain relief
BEST TIME TO TAKE: As needed

Mother Nature's Healthier Alternative to Aspirin

A traditional Japanese food, nattokinase is an enzyme derived from fermenting soy beans with the fungus known as *Bacillus subtilis natto*. It has been used as a traditional meal as far back as 1600. It wasn't until 1987 that its clot-busting and cardio-protective qualities were discovered. To appreciate and trust its true value as an aspirin alternative, you need to understand how blood clotting works.

Blood clots themselves aren't inherently risky. Their formation is the result of a chemical cascade by which a blood compound known as fibrinogen is converted into fibrin. This gives rise to a scaffolding-like structure that halts blood flow, similar to a wash rag blocking the drain.

When we bleed or are injured, the elastic, sticky fibrin molecules gather and thicken near a wound. The entire process is mandatory for healing and is a true testament to our body's natural intelligence. But in excess, blood clots are known as silent killers for their ability to incite heart attack and stroke.

This has doctors on high alert, leading them to aggressively recommend and use aspirin and other blood thinners like Plavix and Coumadin, which dissolve clot-inducing fibrin . . . and unfortunately, many other parts of our body! In an emergency situation, these meds have immense value. But using them daily (outside of an emergency) comes with horrendous side effects. *In fact, repercussions from prescription blood thinners are the leading cause of hospitalization and adverse drug events. That's because they launch an all-out assault on our body's natural healing process and shut down our innate ability to regulate blood clotting.*

Nattokinase to the rescue, it works better, risk-free! But before learning how to use it, you need to understand what causes blood to thicken excessively and dangerously in the first place:

- Dehydration
- High triglycerides (excess sugar consumption)
- Blood glucose greater than 125 mg/dL (normal is 90 to 100 mg/dL)
- Inflammation, which gives rise to compounds known as cytokines

Therefore, the best way to ensure healthy blood is to drink plenty of purified water or spring water, avoid sugar and excess fruits, and take part in weight training to keep inflammation down. In place of risky blood thinners, and outside of an emergency situation, you can use nature's alternative to aspirin to properly regulate the anti-clotting process so that fibrin doesn't form excessive clots.

Nattokinase acts to control fibrin. It keeps it in check by limiting its potential to solidify. This ensures that the clingy compound doesn't yield too many or too few sticky clots! But there's an even more beneficial effect that comes from using nattokinase. It stops inflammation within the arteries, which can lead to total blockage! It's like a Liquid Drano for your pipes!

One of the triggers for clotting is damaged arteries. Once injured, platelets collect within the thin diameter to sooth the inflamed area—like icing a knee. This often occurs due to stress and/or injury caused by sugar and other factors mentioned previously. If in excess, a myriad of sticky, adhesive compounds—including fibrin—begin to congregate on the injured surface within the artery. Over time, this facilitates total blockage, what's technically known as an occlusion.

In a comparison of aspirin and nattokinase, it was found that nature's alternative prevented and reduced the occlusion better and far safer than the over-the-counter blood thinner! This one benefit alone makes nattokinase mandatory for anyone who values total cardiovascular health! Of course, doctors insist that safety might be an issue . . . but that's ludicrous because this supplement has never put anyone in the emergency room!

In fact, one of the most compelling studies showed that its anti-clotting benefits lasted for up to 8 hours after one single dose of 100 mg, without any risk of toxicity or bleeding. Since 1996, these actions have been the subject of dozens of studies around the world that have all come to the same conclusion: 150 to 500 mg/kg of nattokinase per day is a safe and effective, non-toxic anti-clotting compound. Best of all, you won't overdose and you don't need a prescription.[5]

Product Pick

Bulk Supplements Pure Nattokinase Powder 10g
DOSE: 1-2 teaspoons for a 150 lb person
BEST TIME TO TAKE: Morning and night (with or without food)

Chapter 3 Bibliography

(1) Daphne A.RoeM.D. Effects of drugs on nutrition. *Life Sciences.* Volume 15, Issue 7, 1 October 1974, Pages 1219-1234.

(2) M. Michael Wolfe, M.D., David R. Lichtenstein, M.D., and Gurkirpal Singh, M.D. Gastrointestinal Toxicity of Nonsteroidal Antiinflammatory Drugs. *New England Journal of Medicine.* 1999; 340:1888-1899. June 17, 1999

(3) Karen M. Starko. Salicylates and Pandemic Influenza Mortality, 1918–1919 Pharmacology, Pathology, and Historic Evidence. *Clinical Infectious Diseases.* Volume 49, Issue 9, 15 November 2009, Pages 1405–1410.

(4) Irvin Molotsky, Special to the New York Times Published: February 15, 1986. CONSUMER SATURDAY; WARNING ON FLU AND ASPIRIN.

(5) Jang JY1, Kim TS2, Cai J1, Kim J1, Kim Y1, Shin K1, Kim KS1, Park SK3, Lee SP2, Choi EK1, Rhee MH4, Kim YB1. Nattokinase improves blood flow by inhibiting platelet aggregation and thrombus formation. *Laboratory Animal Research.* 2013 Dec;29(4):221-5. Weng Y, Yao J, Sparks S, Wang KY. Nattokinase: An Oral Antithrombotic Agent for the Prevention of Cardiovascular Disease. Arráez-Román D, ed. *International Journal of Molecular Sciences.* 2017;18(3):523. doi:10.3390/ijms18030523.

4

3 Reasons Why We Don't Vaccinate Our Four Children

Bottom line: vaccination is not the same thing as
"immunization." Vaccines don't work. If they did,
there wouldn't be any outbreaks among the vaccinated.

T hree weeks before the birth of our third child, Skyler, my wife Lea-Ann and I were on high alert every day. I tiptoed on eggshells the entire time. Each time my phone buzzed, I thought the baby was coming!

On November 7th, our home birth finally happened. My weight-lifting, pregnant wife (who was featured in *The New York Times,* Huffington Post, CNN, and The London Daily Mail for being a super-fit mom) messaged, "It's time."

"Oh shit! I'll be there in 4 minutes," I texted back from The People's Chemist bunker in Los Angeles.

"The midwives are on the way, right!?" I asked in a near panic.

After rushing through the front door, I yanked out the hose and adapter, air pump, tub, and slip cover—items we always used during our home births. Hauling ass, I left a sloppy trail of water down the hallway to our bedroom from my previous test run days earlier. Pregnancy always gets me nervous.

After all, I'm just a chemist—not a midwife, doctor, doula, or anything associated with birthing a child. As a student of measurable and predictable outcomes, I examine all things relentlessly and intently. I leave nothing to my imagination and follow everything down to its simplest form. I probe until I can define the mystery with a simplicity that baffles others.

But that approach only works with chemical reactions and medicine.

Pregnancy keeps me in a constant state of bewilderment. It might as well be magic. The entire process is like an algebraic equation you can only follow for so long before you get lost in its complexity. Therefore, my philosophy during home birth is, "Don't interfere."

Within seconds, the tub was ready. I hung the towels neatly over the edge. Organic, Egyptian cotton sheets, gourmet dinner, and a glass of wine awaited mom post-birth.

The midwives knocked on the door.

By 3:00 p.m., the entire family and midwives were circled around the tub like it was a campfire. I gave Lily and Blair a nod of confidence to let them know mom was gonna rock the home birth. The midwife gave us all a few simple instructions. They carried the same underlying message: Don't freak out.

Then time stopped.

One minute I was soothing my kids, the next I was ready to jump in the tub to hold my new baby's head as it transitioned into our world. Then, in another frame, our baby was stuck to Lea-Ann's chest like flung paint.

I froze, waiting to hear a victory cry . . .

At first glance, I was sure we had already met on an emotional level. I felt like I was home. It was like a memory that's *felt*, not remembered. Our newborn was all of us, in one.

A cough came, then a cry followed. Victory!

I don't know what a newborn can or cannot see. But I do know that once the crying started, our new baby looked up at mom and calmed instantly—mom was instinctively safe and familiar.

At 3:46 p.m. Skyler was born.

Blair, my 8-year-old son, said the tub looked like a shark attack.

Pregnancy is unmerited sacrifice. For nine months, the soon-to-be-mother breaks her heart, her brain, and her back to get to that final moment, where she still has to yield a Herculean effort to give life, the way nature intended.

The mother's body is simple yet behaves in complex ways we have yet to understand. It's made only from six elements of the periodic table. Together, these elements form DNA, which conveys instructions for chemical reactions that create skin, lungs, a cage of ribs for protection, a placenta, umbilical cord, and everything else that make up a human being in only nine months.

During birth, Mom's body becomes the baby's. If nature had to choose between the two who survives, it usually picks the baby. Every fiber of mom's muscle is directed to this one singular moment of delivering the baby, safely, the way nature intended. Only the strongest women can do it with grace. (I've had the privilege of seeing my wife do it four times, as of the writing of this book!)

In return, I've always tried to contribute by being vigilant about our kids' health and wellness. That started with our first daughter, Lily, when Lea-Ann asked me, "Are we going to vaccinate?"

At the time, I was just out of graduate school and working as a bench chemist for Big Pharma. I had access to every medical and chemistry journal I needed to begin a relentless examination of vaccines. Our biggest concern was whether or not vaccines were safe and effective. And of course, if we decided to opt out, were we contributing to a breakdown in "herd immunity?"

Herd Immunity: Why It Doesn't Hold Up

Herd immunity is a hypothesis plucked out of an old college text book. It states that large groups of immune people can protect those who are immune compromised or unvaccinated. In other words, herd immunity serves as a human shield—a type of immunity—for "at-risk" individuals. Without question, vaccines are said to induce it. But remember, it's only a hypothesis . . . as old as 1840! It has never been proven.

To test herd immunity, you simply have to monitor a highly vaccinated (or even naturally-immune) group for an outbreak. If even one person among the herd is infected and there's a spread—then obviously, herd immunity doesn't work. This is exactly what has been observed.

In Corpus Christi, where the vaccine rate was 99%, measles was undeterred. Scientists writing for *The New England Journal of Medicine* documented the spread of an outbreak among adolescents who had received their shots. The scientists concluded that, "outbreaks of measles can occur in secondary schools, even when more than 99 percent of the students have been vaccinated and more than 95 percent are immune."[1]

Echoing these findings, *The American Journal of Public Health* showed a 98% vaccine rate at a Massachusetts high school. This high rate didn't stop a measles outbreak from erupting among the heavily vaccinated "herd."

Proponents of herd immunity usually insist that outbreaks should be met with yet *more* vaccines, reaching as high as 100% . . . but that's

no longer herd immunity, that's vaccine-induced protection, by definition. Even then, the herd is still vulnerable! And by that point,
you've taken away people's freedom.[2]

In Illinois the Centers for Disease Control and Prevention
(CDC) documented an outbreak despite a 100% vaccine rate in a
high school in Sangamon County. In *Emerging Infectious Diseases*,
scientists discovered whooping cough outbreaks among fully
"immunized" populations of children as well. Their research—published by the CDC—found that, "Vaccinated adolescents and adults
may serve as reservoirs for silent infection and become potential
transmitters to unprotected infants."[3]

You can go as far back as the first test tube and find these same
results, repeated numerous times among different "herds." That's
because herd immunity (as well as vaccine-induced immunity) does
not fully exist outside of textbooks and pharmaceutical propaganda. In other words, you could vaccinate EVERYONE and there
could still be an outbreak.

Ignoring or refusing to learn the facts when outbreaks arise,
health officials are quick to state that this vaccine failure is due to a
breakdown in "herd immunity." Doctors parrot it, too, without even
looking at the research. They say it's happening more often nation-
wide as states make it easier for parents to opt out of vaccinations.

Like argumentative apes, pro-vaccine parents and their physicians start pounding their chests in favor of such statements. More
incredulously, they attack anti-vaccine parents, accusing them of
"putting vaccinated kids at risk due to a breakdown in herd immunity." This is fuzzy logic. And it's borderline stupid. After all, if vaccines truly worked, why would vaccinated kids be at risk? Isn't the
vaccine supposed to protect them?

Ultimately, the facts are clear. Senselessly jabbing tribes of kids with dozens of new-fangled shots isn't going to help anyone. Herd immunity is nothing more than a silly catch-phrase—spawned by those who profit from vaccines—used to scare and bully parents into vaccinating their children.

If pro-vaccine advocates, the media, and doctors truly cared about protecting kids, they'd stop using an unproven hypothesis like herd immunity to question parents who opt out. Instead, a more level-headed approach would be to question the obvious factors that are detracting from our children's health:

- A lack of herd immunity
- Waning vaccine efficacy
- Vaccine failure
- The spread of disease by the vaccinated

Healthy skepticism can go a long way in asking the obvious question: Are vaccines safe and effective for my kids?

My wife Lea-Ann and I discovered three solid reasons to avoid vaccines altogether.

Reason #1: Vaccination Does Not Always Mean "Immunization"

The two words are NOT synonymous. It's widely believed that vaccines work by triggering immunity. When the body is injected with weak or dead infectious agents (i.e., the vaccine), it's thought that the appropriate immune defense is triggered. That's why these shots are often and incorrectly referred to as "immunizations."

Believing that vaccination is the same thing as immunization, many people reference the polio vaccine and its so-called history of eradicating the paralyzing disease. However, when you look past the industry-funded hype, the argument doesn't hold up. In fact, it proves that sometimes a vaccine can cause the very illness it's trying to prevent!

Polio is the most feared childhood illness. It has caused paralysis and death throughout much of human history. Its mere mention inspires terrifying images of crippled children and the Iron Lung. However, these associations are more the result of Pharma-inspired indoctrination than actual polio risk.

In 1910 the world experienced a dramatic increase in polio. This spike in illness was the driving force behind the great race toward the development of a polio vaccine. Mounting public fear became the perfect sales opportunity for drug makers working alongside the government (as usual). Here's how the scheme played out.

Starting in the early 1940's, the March Of Dimes (a "non-profit" organization set up courtesy of the U.S. government) began grooming the public with a manipulative vaccine marketing campaign. Feeding everyone gruesome images of crippled children, they used sensationalist publicity to gain public favor of vaccines. (This was prior to a single vaccine ever being developed or even studied.) Essentially, the March of Dimes fabricated an epidemic that had not yet occurred to win favor for a remedy (vaccine).

Once put into a fearful polio frenzy, people were emotionally powerless to resist. The well-planned front group began siphoning tax dollars away from the government and towards its own pharmaceutical companies in the name of polio immunization—a perceived remedy by the public. Nine million dollars of government money (worth a hundred million today) was doled out for "successful immunization." It was the perfect crime—scare the masses, use tax dollars to fund vaccine makers, make millions in sales. (As you'll see, they still use the same heist today to make billions worldwide.)

In 1953, as planned, the first official polio vaccine was developed and served up to a ravenous public. But the vaccine came too late and was no longer needed. Thanks to improvements in hygiene, sanitation, and nutrition, the rates of polio infection plummeted before vaccine intervention began.

Infection rates also dropped for the Black Plague and many other horrific illnesses for which vaccines were never developed! These diseases were slowly eradicated naturally through a change in human habits that favored better nutrition, hygiene and natural immunity. This fact has been well documented, but always ignored. Even the CDC acknowledged the phenomenon, stating, "The 19th century shift in population from country to city that accompanied industrialization and immigration led to overcrowding in poor housing served by inadequate or nonexistent public water supplies and waste-disposal systems. These conditions resulted in repeated outbreaks of cholera, dysentery, TB, typhoid fever, influenza, yellow fever, and malaria. By 1900, however, the incidence of many of these diseases had begun to decline because of public health improvements, implementation of which continued into the 20th century. Local, state, and federal efforts to improve sanitation and hygiene reinforced the concept of collective "public health" action (e.g., to prevent infection by providing clean drinking water)." Even today, the risk of paralysis from polio infection is still only 1% of those infected, just like it was in the early 1950s despite the media insisting there was an "epidemic." [4, 5]

Still, mass vaccination continued in the 1950s, thanks to the March of Dimes draining the government of money. As polio became less common, many people falsely praised the vaccines—not better hygiene, nutrition, or sanitation—for its defeat. In time, the vaccine was celebrated for its so-called ability to eliminate the paralyzing virus, while the drug's side effects were ignored, buried, and forgotten.

In time, researchers around the world began learning of the drug's notorious side effects, one of which was polio itself. In other words, they noticed the "medicine" was causing the very disease it was intended to protect against.

The Medical Journal of Australia discovered "the relation of prophylactic [preventive] inoculations [polio vaccines] to the onset of poliomyelitis [polio]" as far back as 1951 during early testing. In their research they found increased polio outbreaks among the "immunized." [6]

In 2004 the World Health Organization (WHO) announced that despite a three billion dollar effort to vaccinate as many people as possible, "ten previously polio-free countries across Africa have now been reinfected." The United States showed the same trend. To quote the Centers for Disease Control and Prevention, "From 1980 through 1999, a total of 162 confirmed cases of paralytic poliomyelitis were reported, an average of 8 cases per year. . . . The remaining 154 (95%) cases were vaccine-associated paralytic polio (VAPP) caused by live oral polio vaccine." [7]

Eerily similar to the March of Dimes heist in the 1950s, the Bill and Melinda Gates Foundation has marched off with over *eight billion dollars* by convincing foreign governments like Africa and India to foot the bill for more polio vaccines. In 2007 Reuters published "Nigeria Fights Rare Vaccine-Derived Polio Outbreak," showing how the vaccine itself ignited outbreaks of polio in Nigeria, Chad, and Angola. [8]

According to *The Indian Journal of Medical Ethics,* the polio vaccine program launched by Bill Gates paralyzed 47,500 children in 2011 alone. Indian doctors pleaded, "clinically indistinguishable from polio paralysis, non-polio acute flaccid paralysis was directly proportional to doses of oral polio received." In other words, the more people who got the shots, the more cases of paralysis the country suffered from.[9]

The data is clear. Using the polio vaccine to defend vaccination for its ability to immunize is a weak argument. If you dig even deeper, you can also trace the vaccine to other health complications like cancer and immune deficiency. Pushing for mass vaccination is not only ignorant, it's criminal.

Today's vaccines are, by definition, a crapshoot. Just like with polio, the whooping cough vaccination came too late. Between 1900 and 1935, mortality rates due to whooping cough dropped by 79% in the United States. Yet the vaccine intended to eliminate it (DTP and DTaP) wasn't introduced until 1940.

Today those who have been "immunized" for pertussis are the most susceptible to whooping cough. Researchers with the CDC publicly stated in 2002, "the number of infants dying from whooping cough is rising, despite record high vaccination levels." In 2009 *The Atlanta Journal-Constitution* recognized the trend as well. In an article titled, "Whooping Cough Vaccine not as Powerful as Thought," the publication highlighted a recent cluster of 18 whooping cough-infected students. Seventeen of those students—95% of those infected—had been immunized with five doses of DTaP vaccine.[10]

The measles vaccine shows the same paltry results. In 1957 the Measles, Mumps, and Rubella (MMR) shot became widely used in an effort to eradicate these three diseases. The CDC insisted the vaccine would eliminate mumps in the United States by the year 2010. But rather than preventing mumps and measles, the MMR shot has actually caused widespread epidemics. Outbreaks have become the norm. Those who have suffered the most were "vaccinated."

Between 1983 and 1990, there was a 423% increase in measles cases among vaccinated individuals. In 2006 the largest mumps outbreak in twenty years occurred. Among those infected, 63% were "immunized," as shown by Neil Z. Miller in *Vaccines: Are They Really Safe and Effective?* Others found similar results. In *The Journal of Infectious Diseases,* scientists from Vanderbilt University School of Medicine wrote, "Vaccine failure accounted for a sustained mumps outbreak in a highly vaccinated population."

In his book, *How to Raise a Healthy Child In Spite of Your Doctor,* the late Dr. Robert Mendelsohn, MD, warned parents that vaccinated individuals are 14 times more likely to contract mumps than unvaccinated individuals are.

Over time, these stunning vaccine failures led the Iowa Department of Public Health to conclude, ". . . Our most important public health tool against this disease—2 doses of MMR vaccine—is not providing the necessary levels of protection to control mumps in the U.S. population." Even the Mayo Clinic, which is a bastion of mainstream medicine, states, "vaccine failure has become increasingly apparent."[11]

The flu vaccine has proven to be just as worthless. In 2007 the CDC reported it had "no or low effectiveness" against influenza or influenza-like illnesses. The data showed the flu vaccine protected no more than 14% of those who received it. This wasn't some fluke, either. The vaccine is rarely any more effective than that.

Even *The New York Times* reported, "The influenza vaccine, which has been strongly recommended for people over 65 for more than four decades, is losing its reputation as an effective way to ward off the virus."[12]

Vaccine science has quite a bit of catching up to do before it even remotely resembles the truth. If we are going to jab our children, then we at least need to know how these drugs work, so that we can better understand their efficacy and safety. Until then, vaccine science is still experimental. Confirming this, The World Health Organization (WHO) wrote, "To generate vaccine mediated protection is a complex challenge. Currently available vaccines have largely been developed empirically, with little or no understanding how they activate the immune system."[13]

Vaccine failure isn't a scientific quandary or a mystery. It's easy to understand when you use uncommon sense. The immune system is programmed to recognize and attack invaders that come through the biological "front door," not the skin. (The "front door" is comprised of the nose, mouth, and eyes.) This is especially true for young children—their immune system simply does not recognize biological invaders that come in through the skin (including weak or dead infectious agents contained in a vaccine). In *Immunization, Vaccines and Biologicals,* the WHO found, "Children under two years of age do not consistently develop immunity following vaccination."[14]

Doctors who do their homework understand that vaccines are ineffective. Dr. Ira Goodman, MD, FACS, ABIHM, a surgeon from Loyola Medical School, is one of them. Through email correspondence, he told me he is against vaccines simply because "they don't work!"

Bottom line: vaccination is not the same thing as "immunization." Vaccines don't work. If they did, there wouldn't be any outbreaks among the vaccinated.

Instead of admitting that vaccines don't offer protection, health officials and pharmaceutical companies continue to push for MORE VACCINES as the solution! When you consider the growing history of vaccine failure—and the number of outright toxins contained in these experimental concoctions—the implications for public health are chilling.

Reason #2: Injecting Toxins into Kids is Risky

Many parents insist that because *they* were safely vaccinated as kids, then surely their own children can get shots. This would be true if the vaccines of today were the same as they were decades ago—and used on the same schedule—but of course, they're not. It's ludicrous to think otherwise.

In 1960 an average of three vaccines were given to children. By 1983 this number shot up 800% to 24 doses! Today it's a staggering 49 doses of 14 different vaccines, as recommended by the CDC. That's three times more than any other industrialized nation. Meanwhile, our kids still carry the most illnesses. The culprit? Vaccine toxins.

According to fact sheets released by the CDC and the FDA, vaccines today are brimming with toxins. These include dozens of chemicals, heavy metals, and allergens—as well as the very objectionable monkey kidney cells (Vero cells) and aborted fetal tissue. Sorry, but I have no interest in mainlining these toxic substances into my vulnerable children in the name of "prevention."

Formaldehyde is just one of many questionable chemicals found in vaccines. According to the FDA, "Excessive exposure to formaldehyde may cause cancer." To date, childhood cancer rates like leukemia are skyrocketing along with the number of formalde-hyde-rich vaccines.

The industry covers up this risk by assuring parents that formalde-hyde is naturally produced by the body and that it's completely safe. This is nothing more than hot air—it offers absolutely zero proof of safety and is a total injustice to vulnerable young children. Just because your body produces something doesn't mean you can drink it, eat it, or inject it. It's completely asinine to think otherwise.

For example, the body produces hydrochloric acid (HCL) for digestion. The stomach produces epithelial cells that churn out bicarbonate to neutralize the acerbic compound. Drinking it, eating it, or injecting it would be life-threatening—just like stabbing your-self with formaldehyde can cause leukemia or other forms of cancer years later.

Is anybody using their brain here?

The National Toxicology Program and Department of Health and Human Services countered the absurdity of insisting formalde-hyde is safe. In their report to doctors, they stated, "Formaldehyde is known to be a human carcinogen based on sufficient evidence of carcinogenicity from studies in humans and supporting data on mechanisms of carcinogenesis. Formaldehyde was first listed in the Second Annual Report on Carcinogens in 1981 as reasonably antic-ipated to be a human carcinogen based on sufficient evidence from studies in experimental animals. Since that time, additional cancer studies in humans have been published, and the listing status was changed to known to be a human carcinogen in the Twelfth Report on Carcinogens (2011)." [15]

Another deadly player in the cocktail of chemical preservatives in vaccines is 2-phenoxyethanol. The FDA warns: "It can depress the central nervous system and may cause vomiting and diarrhea, which can lead to dehydration in infants." The Material Safety Data Sheet (MSDS) cautions that the vaccine additive is: "Very hazardous in case of skin contact (irritant), of ingestion, of inhalation."

Singling out the common preservatives used today, *The Medical Science Monitor* highlighted to doctors, "None of the compounds commonly used as preservatives in US licensed vaccine/biological preparations can be considered an ideal preservative, and their ability to fully comply with the requirements of the US Code of Federal Regulations (CFR) for preservatives is in doubt." Adding to the assault, mercury toxicity is lurking nearby in select shots via thimerosal.[16]

Thimerosal is a mercury-containing organic compound (i.e., a preservative) that serves as an antiseptic and antifungal agent. It's used in vaccines as a way of safeguarding against vial contamination. But is it safe for humans to inject into their bodies?

The Centers of Disease Control (CDC) and the FDA insist that thimerosal is safe when used in doses found in vaccines. Taking a pragmatic approach over a scientific one, the status quo insists, "The active form of mercury in vaccines is different than that found in contaminated fish," and "only in trace amounts." True. But both forms are toxic. These government agencies will also parrot The American Academy of Pediatrics who chirp, "The continued benefits of thimerosal use in vaccine manufacturing clearly outweigh any perceived risks."

You can't make informed decisions about thimerosal based on these ridiculous statements. Parents who do are in for a wake-up call. A lifetime of unimaginable pain, suffering, isolation, and madness are lurking nearby for those who choose to play roulette with the silvery sludge. Here's what's not being shown to parents . . .

The last entity to fund a thimerosal study in the United States was Eli Lilly, back in 1929. They're not even a health agency; they're a pharmaceutical drug company. That hardly offers proof of safety and efficacy. Their test churned out horrific results, showing that 100% of the kids jabbed with trace amounts of Merthiolate—the trade name for thimerosal—died from meningitis. How could that possibly be considered safe? Meanwhile, the Pharma-funded authors (using ghostwriting) still concluded that there was no causal association between mercury in vaccines and harm.

In time, the devastating effects could no longer be ignored. On January 5, 1982, the FDA published its notice of proposed rule-making regarding thimerosal. Their scientific panel's opinions and recommendations were the culmination of five years of research concerning the potential hazards and safety of thimerosal. Published in the Federal Register, the panel concluded:

> "At the cellular level, thimerosal has been found to be more toxic for human epithelial cells in vitro than mercuric chloride, mercuric nitrate, and merbromim (mercurochrome)."

> "Exhibit 34 (Exhibit ELI-512). The FDA specifically found that thimerosal was significantly more toxic for living tissue than it was for the bacteria it was supposed to kill."

> "It was found to be 35.3 times more toxic for embryonic chick heart tissue than for staphylococcus aureus [top killer in hospitals today]."

> "The Panel concludes that thimerosal is not safe for [over-the-counter] topical use because of its potential for cell damage if applied to broken skin and its allergy potential."

The FDA's findings clearly should have settled the matter—that thimerosal is not safe for humans, let alone children, to use.

In 2001 the pharmaceutical industry promised removal of thimerosal from vaccines. Sadly, nine vaccine shots still contained the metallic poison in the year 2016. The irony of promising to remove a "safe" preservative is proof that thimerosal is risky. If you need more proof, a little math goes a long way.

The Environmental Protection Agency (EPA)'s acceptable dose for mercury is 0.1 microgram per kilogram of body weight, per day. Running simple conversions, this means a 10-pound baby who gets jabbed with a thimerosal-rich vaccine receives an insurmountable 55 times the safe upper limit for mercury exposure. For an adult given the same injection, that'd be four times the safe supper limit!

Pleading for thimerosal removal, Congressman Dan Burton wrote to the Secretary of Health and Human Services to make his case. He insisted, "During a review required by the Food and Drug Modernization Act, it was learned that infants receive more mercury [from thimerosal] in the first six months of life than is considered safe according to federal guidelines. For a twelve-to-fourteen month old child receiving vaccines on the Universal Childhood Immunization Schedule as they are typically delivered (four to six shots in one doctor visit), they may receive forty or more times the amount of mercury than is considered safe according to Environmental Protection Agency (EPA) guidelines. The EPA guidelines were confirmed to be accurate through an independent evaluation conducted by the National Research Council (NRC)."

If you read the vaccine package inserts, the danger of thimerosal becomes even more apparent. The DPT (diphtheria, pertussis, and tetanus) vaccine maker Sanofi Pasteur warned, "A review by the

Institute of Medicine (IOM) found evidence for a causal relation between tetanus toxoid and both brachial neuritis and Guillain-Barré syndrome [pain and loss of nerve and motor function]."

Makers of the Tripedia vaccine for DTaP (which is rich in thimerosal) stated, "The vaccine is formulated without preservatives, but contains a trace amount of thimerosal [(mercury derivative), (≤0.3 µg mercury/dose)] from the manufacturing process."

Certain negative outcomes are so frequent that the manufacturer had to list them in a public warning:

- Sudden Infant Death Syndrome (SIDS)
- Anaphylactic reaction
- Cellulitis (a bacterial skin infection)
- Autism
- Convulsion/Seizures
- Brain dysfunction
- Low muscle tone and strength
- Nerve damage
- Hyperventilation/apnea

In his extremely well-researched book *Thimerosal: Let The Science Speak: The Evidence Supporting the Immediate Removal of Mercury—a Known Neurotoxin—from Vaccines*, Robert F. Kennedy Jr. showed there's more global scientific muscle power than what it took to build the space station proving that thimerosal is ruining the health of our nation. And yet, with unconstrained malice and well-calculated schemes, Pharma continues to profit by selling cheaper, mercury-rich vaccines in 40 other countries. Once the country's citizens are riddled with shots, research shows that continents like Africa, as well as citizens living near the Amazon river, are forever scarred from neurological damage.

Thimerosal has an evil twin, making the combo more dangerous than the individual ingredients. Accompanying mercury is aluminum. Brought to the attention of doctors by *Nature,* evidence from the *Journal of Exposure Science and Environmental Epidemiology* found that both thimerosal at small concentrations and aluminum are neurotoxic.[17]

The journal insisted, "In this regard, aluminum adsorbed vaccines caused a transient rise in brain tissue of mice. Indeed, in vitro work showed that adjuvant-Al [aluminum] at levels comparable to those administered to adults can kill motor neurons." The outcome was neurotoxicity, which leads to a higher risk of receiving special education services and nerve cell deterioration, causing memory loss and possibly dementia later in life.

Consistent with these observations, an elaborate toxicological report for aluminum prepared by the Agency for Toxic Substances and Disease Registry (ATSDR) reported that, "There is a rather extensive database on the oral toxicity of aluminum in animals. These studies clearly identify the nervous system as the most sensitive target of aluminum toxicity."

In *Current Medicinal Chemistry,* scientists warned that despite 90 years of widespread use of aluminum adjuvants, "their precise mechanism of action remains poorly understood." Digging deeper into aluminum toxicity, they showed that aluminum presented in vaccines "carries a risk for autoimmunity, long-term brain inflammation and associated neurological complications and may thus have profound and widespread adverse health consequences. The widely accepted notion of aluminum adjuvant safety does not appear to be firmly established in the scientific literature and, as such, this absence may have lead to erroneous conclusions regarding the significance of these compounds in the etiologies of many common neurological disorders."[18]

The assault from chemical threats isn't the only concern. Many vaccines are spiked with antibiotics like neomycin, polymyxin B, streptomycin, and gentamicin—all of which can set off allergic reactions and threaten liver and kidney health. None of the these medications are even approved by the FDA for children.

Interested in clinical observations from medical doctors, I reached out to Dr. Suzanne Humphries, MD, to express my concern as a chemist and father. She was adamant in her position: "Vaccines put children most at risk for a form of kidney disease called nephrotic syndrome. This can be caused by a common ingredient—Bovine Serum Albumin. Doctors just give children steroids to suppress the symptoms, never reporting it or knowing what the cause was."

These were some damn good reasons for my wife and I to avoid vaccinating our kids. Doctors still insist that the benefits outweigh these toxicity risks. But that would only be true if vaccination offered guaranteed immunization. It doesn't. That said, why would anyone risk exposing their kids to toxins when there's no guaranteed benefit— especially when natural immunity is available to protect you?

Reason #3: Kids Can Build Immunity Naturally

It's a fact of life: invisible threats are everywhere. We're all at risk from various "biological nasties," germs, and foreign invaders. A single gram of feces can contain more than 10 million viruses, 1 million bacteria, 1,000 parasite cysts and 100 parasite eggs. From the hands we shake, to the water we drink and the mats we wrestle on, nowhere is safe . . . unless you've built up natural immunity in your body. This firewall acts as our God-given protection from the incalculable number of threatening microorganisms.

Professor Sven Gard, member of the Staff of Professors of the Royal Caroline Institute, identified the importance of our body's ability to protect itself. Speaking to The Nobel Prize Committee, he warned that "The capacity of developing [natural] immunity is one of the most important means of defense, of decisive importance for the survival of the individual and the species." Over time, some of the world's top scientific minds have begun focusing on demystifying the mysterious complexities of self-protection (i.e., natural immunity) and how to harness it.

One of the most interesting discoveries in natural immunity occurred in 1908. Venerable scientists Ilya Mechnikov and Paul Ehrlich revealed how our immune system is armed with a special set of destroyer cells. Studying simple-celled aquatic life, they observed how phagocytes eradicate infection by digesting them and subsequently eliminating them. Robust and resilient, the average person has about six billion of these armed sentries ready to attack. [19]

In 2011 Bruce Beutler and Jules Hoffmann observed that the immune system is pre-programmed to identify self and non-self. This discovery single-handedly proved humans are hardwired to build immunity, outside of vaccination. This work paved the way for future scientists to discover how our body thwarts numerous types of pathogenic microorganisms including bacteria, virus, fungi, and parasites. [20]

Arguing in favor of vaccines, pro-vaccine parents insist that newborns lack immunity. Pushing for more shots for everyone else, they insist that herd immunity is the best protection for the young and unvaccinated. They couldn't be more wrong.

Natural immunity is a biological gift from our mothers and DNA. According to more award-winning science, natural protection is fully developed during the earliest stages of life. First, it's passed from mom and after a few weeks or months, it's fully developed in newborns. Plus, thanks to "immunological memory," natural immunity lasts a lifetime. This explains why we're protected from the millions of other known microorganisms that we don't have vaccines for!

Scientist Sir Peter Medawar and co-workers presented their experimental evidence to prove the validity of immunological memory in 1960. The Nobel Prize committee awarded them for their work, stating: "Immunity is our perhaps most important defense against a hostile surrounding world. By penetrating analysis of existing data and brilliant deduction, and by painstaking experimental research you have unveiled a fundamental law governing the development and maintenance of this vital mechanism. On behalf of the Caroline Institute, I extend to you our warm congratulations, and ask you to receive the Nobel Prize for Physiology or Medicine from the hands of His Majesty the King." [21]

To this day, Medawar's observation has been abundantly confirmed. His work was the foundation for developing medicine to shut down organ rejection among transplant patients. Otherwise, immunological memory would work against patients and attack foreign tissue as if it was being infected from outside threats. Medawar's observation also put a spotlight on misguided vaccine supporters who insist that vaccination is the only road to protection form childhood diseases.

Natural immunity works—but only if you support it with proper hygiene, sanitation, and what I call "nutrient logic." Without phagocytes, immunological memory, and the ability to identify self from non-self, the power of natural immunity is diminished. This forgotten logic dictates that today's health and immunity threats are simply the result of gaping nutrient deficiencies. By failing to give your body the right nutrients, you deny the body its ability to grow, build immunity, and protect itself.

Nutrient logic addresses the deficiency by filling the nutritional void or malnutrition to restore proper cellular and immune function. Better than a pharmacist doling out meds, the body becomes its own "pharmacy" by producing custom-made medicine to enhance survival, through nutrient logic.

The process is as simple and logical as resurrecting a dying, sun-deprived plant with sun exposure and water, which initiates photosynthesis for the production of life-giving glucose. That same innate intelligence guides our own health and immunity when we obtain essential molecules—i.e., nutrients—from nature.

Just as hand washing and soap saved millions from infant mortality caused by unwanted intruders in a hospital setting, nutrient logic boosts our natural defenses. Reams of scientific data show that natural birth, breastfeeding, and cod liver oil (Norwegians' mainstay of health) are among the most important strategies for building and protecting our children's natural defenses.

Finding the proper cod liver oil can be challenging. This stems from supplement hucksters who don't know the difference between naturally occurring nutrients and those made in a lab (synthetic) or what I refer to here as "processed," for simplification. Make the wrong choice and you might be harming yourself with laboratory mimics of nature.

The best way to find the right cod liver oil is to know the difference between processed and unprocessed oils. Once mindful of the two, you can protect your kids from the side effects associated with choking down imposters: poor energy and focus, calcification leading to heart failure, and cancer. To understand the differences, you have to go way back to simpler times when there wasn't a barrage of choices, misinformation, and Big Pharma to screw it all up.

The use of cod liver oil in medicine has been documented as far back as Hippocrates and the Roman naturalist, Pliny. Safe and effective, this oil was also used by the Vikings as early as the 700s to 1100.

As cod liver oil continued its reign as a natural remedy through harsh winters, Dr. Ruth A. Guy published *The History of Cod Liver Oil* in 1923.[22] This was among the first and most extensive documents showing positive, measurable results associated with using cod liver oil, observed by physicians in Germany, Holland, England, and France. Published in *The American Journal of Diseases of Children,* Guy's article documented numerous cod liver oil cures for:

- Rickets
- Rheumatism
- Gout
- Bone and joint diseases
- Osteomalacia (softening of the bones)
- Arrhythmia
- Invasive blood clotting
- Many forms of tuberculosis

Back then, cod liver oil was unprocessed. If you're going to consume cod liver oil today, then you'll want to find a product that's been proven beneficial—unprocessed cod liver oil. Today you have to look for "extra-virgin" cod liver oil.

Modern-day laboratory testing methods reveal the contents of extra-virgin cod liver oil. These testing methods show that extra-virgin cod liver oil is unadulterated, delivering a one-of-a-kind blend of fatty acids and micronutrients in doses and ratios that are ultra-safe and extremely therapeutic. Specifically, these medicinal compounds are:

- Omega-3 fats EPA and DHA
- Naturally occurring vitamin A
- Naturally occurring vitamin D
- Naturally occurring vitamin E
- And more

Unfortunately, you can't get these healing ingredients from a processed oil. Wanting to piggy-back off the success of extra-virgin cod liver oil and its synergistic ingredients, numerous knock-offs have been spawned by the dietary supplement industry and Big Pharma. Today you can choose among a vast array of processed cod liver oils that have synthetic "vitamins" tossed in for "good measure" or worse, pharmaceutical omega-3 fatty acids like Lovaza and Vascepa. Stripped down, these wannabes don't confer the same healthy benefits as extra-virgin cod liver oil.

There are typically four types of fish oils to choose from:

- Extra-virgin cod liver oil (unprocessed)
- Cod liver oil (if it's not labeled as extra-virgin, then it's processed)
- Omega-3 fish oils
- Prescription omega-3 PUFA (Polyunsaturated Fatty Acids)

There's always argumentative tripe about which cod liver oil or fish oil is best. Pharmaceutical industry slaves and wannabe doctors bicker about what the "blend" should contain or why their omega-3 "fish oil" is superior. In the same breath, they're quick to sell you their own special oil or vitamin. Or they insist we need to overdose on isolated or individual, synthetic ingredients to raise our blood levels to procure health. Hell, the medical industry has even devised blood tests and artificially raised the standards of most nutrients in an attempt to make us think we're all deficient, so they can get us hooked on their unique product.

I say—they're all apes. Screw them all.

Comparatively, the evidence shows (just like it did a hundred years ago) that extra-virgin (unprocessed) cod liver oil works vastly better than any of the the processed versions. It also works better than the high-dose, pharmaceutical mimics most people know as omega-3 fatty acids, vitamin A, vitamin D, and pharmaceutical grade omega-3 oils. That's good news, because it means consumers can ditch most vitamin pills and potions and simply rely on old-fashioned, extra-virgin cod liver oil.

In stark contrast, vapid, sterile ingredients stirred into processed cod liver or highly distilled or lab-derived "omega-3" oils are just cheap decoys of extra-virgin cod liver oil. Commonly found on the shelves of grocery stores and at Whole Foods, these unhealthy and sometimes toxic products (toxic due to abnormally high amounts of ingredients)—lead to "hypervitaminosis"—i.e., poisoning by vitamins. These toxic vitamins should be avoided at all costs. You'd get more benefit from sniffing ether.

Fake cod liver oil knock-offs won't yield healthy outcomes. In the worst case scenario, they'll harm your health, which is why I'd never let my family choke them down. Regarding the side effects caused by prescription omega-3 fats, the FDA published that, "adverse events reported by 1 or more patients from 22 clinical studies are:"

"BODY AS A WHOLE: enlarged abdomen, asthenia, body odor, chest pain, chills, suicide, fever, generalized edema, fungal infection, malaise, neck pain, neoplasm, rheumatoid arthritis, sudden death, and viral infection."

"CARDIOVASCULAR SYSTEM: arrhythmia, bypass surgery, cardiac arrest, hyperlipidemia, hypertension, migraine, myocardial infarct, myocardial ischemia, occlusion, peripheral vascular disorder, syncope, and tachycardia."

"DIGESTIVE SYSTEM: anorexia, constipation, dry mouth, dysphagia, colitis, fecal incontinence, gastritis, gastroenteritis, gastrointestinal disorder, increased appetite, intestinal obstruction, melena, pancreatitis, tenesmus, and vomiting."

If that isn't crazy enough, the pharmaceutical industry charges up to $500 per month for these risky omega-3 imposters. Fraudulent and criminal, it's business as usual.

In contrast, extra-virgin cod liver oil produces zero side effects, and it's much less expensive. Of course, your insurance company won't pay for this version . . . thanks to the great extortion scam Western Medicine has going on, courtesy of the U.S. Government.

....

Product Pick
Rosita Real Foods Extra-Virgin Cod Liver Oil
DOSE: 1-3 teaspoons daily per 150 lb person
    and 1 teaspoon if under 12 years old
BEST TIME TO TAKE: Anytime

....

The Antibiotic Alternative

As a father, by the time baby number four rolls around, you think you have it all figured out. Your role, as a guy, is simply to stand on the sidelines of birth and make sure mom and baby are comfortable and safe. Then you wait for the big show.

I was as calm as a Buddhist monk sipping beer. We were preparing for another home birth. Been there, done that. We got this. But then. . . . I got a frantic call from my wife. She'd just discovered she had tested positive for Group B strep (GBS) while being pregnant. Aubrey was due in four weeks.

Buddhist monk mode was over. GBS is a type of bacterial infection that can be found in the uterus, placenta, or urinary tract. For many, it's harmless. But if transmitted to a baby during birth, the outcome is a parent's worst nightmare—shock, pneumonia, and/or meningitis.

Like 20-40% of pregnant moms, Lea-Ann was a carrier. As you can imagine, she was distraught. After seven-and-a-half months of doing everything right, suddenly now it seemed like something was terribly wrong. Already in a vulnerable state, Lea-Ann's head was spinning with blame. "How could this have happened?" she wondered.

The possibility of a hospital birth and a sick baby was imminent. I went into chemist mode. We began discussing the options, free of the typical scare tactics from Western Medicine.

The typical protocol for GBS-positive moms is to pump the mother full of IV antibiotics during birth, or perform a C-section. Not on my watch.

A healthy, natural childbirth sets the stage for a healthy future and vice versa. This has been well established. Using antibiotics as "preventive medicine" comes with life-long consequences. It wasn't worth the risk.

Fact is, bacteria is everywhere. Life is essentially water and bacteria. Test for any strain and you can usually find it. Therefore, being afraid of bacteria isn't a healthy life strategy . . . even if that bacteria has a scary name like "GBS" or "Strep B"!

It's extremely rare for a healthy mom to pass GBS onto a healthy baby. Thanks to emergency medicine, it's even more rare for a baby to suffer the worst consequences of GBS. Plus, giving birth in water (i.e., a water birth) adds yet another layer of protection, putting the odds in your favor.

My wife and I both agreed to skip the antibiotics. After all, 50% of the time, they don't even work—and they yield side effects 100% of the time. We got back on track for our home birth plan and aimed for a healthy delivery in water.

I may know about antibiotics, but I have zero clinical experience with Strep B infection. So I arranged to have two superstar midwives by our side to watch closely for signs of GBS upon birth. Decades of wisdom and experience were lined up around the tub!

In the last 50 years, Western Medicine has built a system of blind loyalty to medications. When faced with the unknown—like GBS—we throw medications at the patient like spaghetti on a wall to see what sticks. The benefit is rarely greater than the risk. the superbug scourge (in which bacteria are now learning to evade antibiotics), as well as the side effects to a baby's immune system, the general ineffectiveness of antibiotics, and the wanton overuse of prescription drugs—we're now in the grips of a modern day tragedy. Ignoring these hard truths, hospitals are too quick to slap IVs on mom and baby.

Not in the Ellison household.

Lea-Ann went into labor on Wednesday at 2 p.m. She went to float in our swimming pool to ease the pain. I jumped in with Skyler (who was by now a year old), and we both pondered if it would be a girl or a boy.

I thought back to all the stages Lea-Ann and I had already been through…parents of one kid, then two kids, then three kids, and soon to be four. I remembered our first-born, Lily—who came out of the womb so damn serious and driven, the home birth has paid off in spades only 13 years later. Our second-born, Blair—benevolent, curious, and determined, instantly wrapped his long arms around mom as he came out of the water. Our third-born, Skyler—happy and playful day and night, so active you have to feed him on the run.

All of our children have been resilient survivors and thrivers. All of them were delivered in home births. Who's next? I wondered.

After an hour of labor, it was time to wrap it up. Lea-Ann went inside to sit in the tub. Shortly thereafter, her water broke. Seconds later, she was holding our new baby girl. Gentle and appreciative, our new daughter flailed her petite arms looking for something familiar. Catching her attention, mom's warm skin calmed her instantly. She rested solemnly in mom's arms. Eyes shut, the baby savored the moment and held tight, all her senses life. She startled herself with a cry and quickly embrace. All was fine in the world.

We named her Aubrey.

In that one instant, everything changed. We were now the proud parents of four! A carbon copy of Lea-Ann, Aubrey was born healthy, happy, and full of love. Calm, centered, confident and borderline sassy—she's sure to keep Skyler in check throughout the years.

Antibiotics could have stolen this moment forever. Without signs of infection or a dire need for them, antibiotics are the worst possible meds to take. Using them as preventive medicine is totally unnecessary, because you have no way knowing what strain of bacteria you're even trying to prevent—and therefore have no idea what medication to use, since all antibiotics target different strains.

In life-or-death situations, antibiotics are a luxury. But their wanton overuse is slowly killing us. Not only are they inciting a massive wave of side effects, they're also training bacteria how to evade our most potent medicines. The most common side effects of antibiotics are:

- Dehydration
- Liver and kidney failure
- Nerve damage
- Joint pain
- Anxiety
- Confusion
- Agitation
- Severe depression

If our current use of antibiotics continues at the rate it's been ~~   ~~ all current medications ~~   ~~ World Health Organization (WHO). *Scientific American* reported that many varieties of drug-resistant E. coli have already been discovered in China. Even worse, the resistant super-bacteria is being spread by flies. As this threat of overusing man-made antibiotics increases, our defenses decrease. In time, we could have no defenses left against biological nasties when we truly need them in a life-threatening emergency. If this happens, "our longevity would go back to the Stone Age, where every infection was life threatening," warns the WHO.

Just by looking at the outcome of mass antibiotic use, we can see that antibiotics should never be used as a first line of defense against common illness. This means you must be committed to using natural immune boosters prior to rushing off for meds! When I wrote *Over-The-Counter Natural Cures Expanded,* I taught that the lucky run we've had with prescription antibiotics was over. While they saved us short term, they'll kill us longterm. Now we must rely on our own immune system. To strengthen our natural defenses, we can use natural medicine like andrographis (see *Over-the-Counter Natural Cures Expanded*), which is proven to ward off biological nasties, safely and quickly, without risk. A long history of science has proven its effectiveness against viral infection as well as the flu, strep, and much more. In light of this, I stressed in the book that antibiotics should never be used for:

- Ear infection
- Strep throat
- Flu
- Bee Stings
- Common cold
- Urinary
- Preventive medicine during or after birth in hospital

The Three Most Dangerous Antibiotics

1. Levaquin
2. Vancomycin
3. Bactrim

4 of the Safest Antibiotics

1. Penicillin
2. Amoxicillan
3. Cephalexin (Keflex)
4. Erythromycin

If you must take any of these antibiotics, there are certain things you can do to increase their safety profile: namely, consume them with plenty of purified water, milk thistle, and probiotics, which help rebuild the "good" bacteria in your gut that is destroyed by antibiotics. Also, never consume alcohol while taking antibiotics, as this will just increase the chances of suffering side effects.

The euphoria over antibiotics can be strong, especially after experiencing their amazing ability to rescue a loved one from the grips of a truly life-threatening illness. But we can't let the euphoria overpower our logic and push us to overuse antibiotics. These meds should always be the LAST line of defense, never the first.

Chapter 4 Bibliography

(1) Tracy L. Gustafson, M.D., Alan W. Lievens, M.D., Philip A. Brunell, M.D., Ronald G. Moellenberg, B.S., Christopher M.G. Buttery, M.D., and Lynne M. Sehulster, Ph.D.Measles Outbreak in a Fully Immunized Secondary-School Population. *New England Journal of Medicine.* 1987; 316:771-774. March 26, 1987.

(2) Nkowane BM, Bart SW, Orenstein WA, Baltier M. Measles outbreak in a vaccinated school population: epidemiology, chains of transmission and the role of vaccine failures. *American Journal of Public Health.* 1987;77(4):434-438.

(3) Srugo I, Benilevi D, Madeb R, Shapiro S, Shohat T, Somekh E, et al. Pertussis Infection in Fully Vaccinated Children in Day-Care Centers, Israel. Emerg Infect Dis. 2000;6(5):526-529.

(4) Centers for Disease Control and Prevention. Achievements in Public Health, 1900-1999: Control of Infectious Diseases. https://www.cdc.gov/Mmwr/preview/mmwrhtml/mm4829a1.htm

(5) Miller NZ. *Vaccines—Are They Really Safe and Effective?* Santa Fe, NM, New Atlantean Press, 1992

(6) Mawdsley, Stephen. Balancing Risks: Childhood Inoculations and America's Response to the Provocation of Paralytic Polio. *Social History of Medicine,* Volume 26, Issue 4, 1 November 2013, Pages 759–778.

(7) Fleck F. WHO warns of a polio epidemic in Africa. *BMJ : British Medical Journal.* 2004;328(7455):1513.

(8) MacInnis, Laura. *Nigeria fights rare vaccine-derived polio outbreak.* October 8, 2007.

(9) Vashisht N, Puliyel J. Polio programme: let us declare victory and move on. *Indian Journal of Medical Ethics.* 2012 Apr-Jun;9(2):114-7.

(10) Young, Alison. *Whooping cough vaccine not as powerful as thought.* The Atlanta Journal-Constitution Sunday, March 22, 2009.

(11) Jacobson RM1, Poland GA, Vierkant RA, Pankratz VS, Schaid DJ, Jacobsen SJ, Sauver JS, Moore SB. The association of class I HLA alleles and antibody levels after a single dose of measles vaccine. *Human Immunology.* 2003 Jan;64(1):103-9.

(12) Goodman, Brenda. Doubts Grow Over Flu Vaccine in Elderly. *The New York Times*. Sep. 1, 2008

(13) Stanley A. Plotkin & Walter Orenstein & Paul A. Offit. *Vaccines, 6th Edition*. ISBN: 9780323357616.

(14) http://archives.who.int/vaccines/en/pneumococcus.shtml

(15) 14th Report on Carcinogens. U.S. Department of Health and Human Services released the 14th Report on Carcinogens on November 3, 2016.

(16) Geier DA, Jordan SK, Geier MR. The relative toxicity of compounds used as preservatives in vaccines and biologics. *Medical Science Monitor*. 2010 May;16(5):SR21-7.

(17) José G Dórea and Rejane C Marques. Infants' exposure to aluminum from vaccines and breast milk during the first 6 months. *Journal of Exposure Science and Environmental Epidemiology*. 2010, 20, 598–601.

(18) L. Tomljenovic and C.A. Shaw. Aluminum Vaccine Adjuvants: Are they Safe? Current Medicinal Chemistry, 2011, 18, 2630-2637 0929-8673.

(19) "The Nobel Prize in Physiology or Medicine 1908". *Nobelprize.org*. Nobel Media AB 2014. Web. 24 Aug 2017.

(20) "The 2011 Nobel Prize in Physiology or Medicine—Press Release". *Nobelprize.org*. Nobel Media AB 2014. Web. 24 Aug 2017

(21) "The Nobel Prize in Physiology or Medicine 1960". *Nobelprize.org*. Nobel Media AB 2014. Web. 24 Aug 2017

(22) GUY RA. THE HISTORY OF COD LIVER OIL AS A REMEDY. *The American Journal of Diseases Children*. 1923;26(2):112–116.

How to Get Started on Ditching the Meds

Medications are for sick people,
not those living young.
You can't be healthy and on meds at the same time.

In February 2015 a photo of a dress went viral online. People went nuts over the color of the dress. Endless debate ensued. Viewers obsessed over the question, "What color is the dress?" This idiocy was featured on every news site, written about in *The New York Times,* and even discussed on *CNN.*

"Experts" chimed in with their scientific analysis on what color they thought the dress was . . . and why people were seeing different colors. Some saw gold, some saw blue. I saw fifty shades of "Who-Gives-a-Fuck?"

The drivel about whether the dress was gold or blue proved that the brain can ultimately be your worst enemy—it fools you into seeing what you want to see. This is called "confirmation bias."

Remember that term, because it's the chief weapon Big Pharma uses against you to get you hooked on meds. They know you'll only see what you want to see, as long as you're served the perfect blend of happy music, hypnotic images, and carefully chosen marketing spin.

It's similar to when a five-year-old covers up his eyes and yells, "Nah nah nah! I can't see you!" to his mother who's sitting right in front of him. That's confirmation bias in its earliest form. The child is ignoring that which is right in front of him—usually during a scolding—courtesy of confirmation bias. Adults do the same thing every day when it comes to their prescription meds. The patient only "sees" the ridiculous benefits offered by a drug. They don't see the drug's side effects, the checkbook science, or the fraud running most of the drug industry.

Public relations firms and marketing whizzes for Big Pharma bank on confirmation bias, using it to create insane demands for meds. They know they can leverage it to brainwash millions of people into believing bullshit, despite the stench all around them (from the body count of millions who died from using prescription drugs).

Even some pilots have adhered to confirmation bias. When weather didn't cooperate for them, they refused to accept that it was life-threatening to take off. They ignored the inclement weather hovering above. "I can make it," were the last words of pilots who only saw what they wanted to see—courtesy of confirmation bias.

During the "Dressgate" scandal, very few people saw that the image of the dress was distorted and that technically, it didn't have just one color. It was a fake. There were multiple, computer-generated colors. Yet, subconsciously, people let their brain run amuck and in their haste, they started choosing colors based on obscure bits of information (OBOI). In reality, there should have been more people saying "Who-Gives-a-Fuck?" and going back to living their lives instead of wasting time arguing. When you don't have all the information available, you shouldn't be making decisions about said topic. You should be asking questions.

Writing on the ambiguity of the dress, an article in the *Times* stated that when people only have "obscure bits of information," their brain fills in the gaps and sees what it wants to see based on how it is conditioned. This phenomenon has been tested and verified in many other fields. In the war of marketing and PR, OBOI is used against you.

Ever notice how Big Pharma and Western Medicine uses OBOI? Think of the data you're given. Ever feel like you weren't being given the whole picture from that television ad, social media post, or parroted script from your "robo-doc?" "The benefits outweigh the risks," is a common refrain. But as you know by now, after reading this book, that's total bullshit.

It's conditioning people to take their meds. The media's headlines are trying to sway your mind into accepting an invisible status quo that says prescription drugs are good for you. This is done to condition you via confirmation bias. Don't fall for it.

Ultimately, Big Pharma intentionally creates OBOI to fool the American public from cradle to grave. Starting in school, they train people to engage in an internal dialogue that says, "I need medication to be healthy." By the time they're adults, the technique has already worked—and most people are trained to "follow doctor's orders" without question. This mantra gets seeped into the very core of everyone's consciousness.

Like using only a few pixels on a computer screen to manipulate the color of a dress, Big Pharma uses just enough sound bites (an expert here and a doctor there) to make drugs seem amazing. Then they add in paid celebrities to endorse products they don't have the slightest clue about. This massive business and public relations scam has been going on for ages.

Like Nazi mind control, OBOI gets repeated thousands of times per day on the news, in movies and in commercials, on social media, on the radio, all while slowly gaining power over people's emotions and minds. The results are a slew of hypnotic messages that echo sentiments of, "I need my meds."

Unless you're keenly aware of this stuff, you're probably not in control of your life or your health. These useless, random bits of info have successfully trained Americans to dutifully pop pills at a doctor's every whim. I overcame this scam only after spending years with my head buried inside a library during college and graduate school, and after rewiring my brain.

Most people will defend their confirmation bias all the way to the grave. I've seen it firsthand. Sadly, I've watched people die young from meds before they've ever even considered an alternative (or reading a fucking book).

Before you know it, you're taking blood pressure meds, Lipitor, aspirin, and a fistful of other drugs to offset the side effects of the original drugs you were taking. Never mind that this pharmaceutical merry-go-round is killing thousands of Americans daily, and millions worldwide. Like the pilot who fails to look at inclement weather, the patient fails to look at the rising body count from prescription drugs.

Good news is, you can stop the Nazi mind control crap right now. You don't have to be hypnotized by OBOI. You can simply arm yourself with facts, and be ready to accept them whether your doctor likes them or not. Fortunately, when it comes to science, it only takes one person to verify reproducible results, like an apple falling from a tree. That, in a nutshell, is science. It doesn't require a democracy, a popularity contest, a Photoshopped celebrity, a ghost-written article, or a staff meeting to see if everyone is on board.

Want to free yourself from OBOI? Then ditch the meds (outside of an emergency.) Medications are for sick people, not those living young. You can't be healthy and on meds at the same time. If you go against this, then be prepared to face the consequences. You've been warned!

One individual dies about every five minutes from an "approved" drug—that's almost 300 deaths every day, according to the *Journal of the American Medical Association* (JAMA) and the Institute of Medicine (IOM). The so-called cure is killing people. Most people won't win today's prescription drug battle. If piled up, the corpses from annual drug deaths would reach from Earth up 125,000 feet where Felix Baumgartner made his record-breaking jump from space.

Katrina is one of those rare people who escaped the scourge of OBOI. After freeing herself, her life changed for the better.

Like so many others, Katrina emailed me sharing how drugs had ravaged her health. (She almost became a statistic—another name-less, faceless brick in the growing tower of pharmaceutical deaths.) For 10 years, Katrina was a doctor's punching bag. Weighing in at 276 pounds, she was pummeled by this drug and that drug. When those prescriptions didn't work, the doctor increased the meds— like a fighter throwing more uppercuts—while assuring Katrina "the benefits outweighed the risks."

Sure, Katrina's own bad habits had forced her into the medical boxing ring. Over the phone, she admitted, "I was seriously sick and had been for over a decade from self-inflicting abuse to my body."

It started when she was a kid.

"I've been overweight since I was 8 years old. I ate mostly sugar-coated cereals, chips, and fast food. Of course the weight piled on."

Our sick care system was set up to prey off of this exact scenario. Poisoned by the Standard American Diet (SAD) as kids, adult lives are dominated by poor health. With OBOI dominating their thought process, prescription medications are their first line of defense.

"I was diagnosed with Type 2 diabetes in 2001 at the age of 30. I'm 42 now and was on medicine since the age of 24. When I found The People's Chemist, I was on 9 prescription medicines including the dreaded fat storing medication, insulin! My doctors had diagnosed me with high cholesterol, high triglycerides, high blood pressure, Type 2 diabetes, morbid obesity, and hyperactive thyroid," Katrina wrote.

Despite the barrage of prescription drugs she was taking (per doctor's orders), her health continued to deteriorate. She spoke of the ongoing emotional turmoil she suffered:

"It was a daily struggle being overweight. Every minute was a challenge."

"I didn't know what to do."

Like a world champion heavyweight about to embark on an epic comeback, Katrina did the only thing she could. She dug deep and found a constellation of courage that gave her the strength to keep fighting.

"One night I was surfing the web for celebrity gossip and stumbled across The People's Chemist. I weighed 276 lbs at the time. The heaviest I had ever been. I read with intent and decided to ditch the meds."

Katrina started her comeback first by making the decision to ditch the meds. When you have the toughness and power of a mom who wants a better life for herself and daughter, nothing can hold you back—especially when you've been taking rounds out of sheer frustration of broken promises, courtesy of Western Medicine's OBOI.

Katrina was in smash mode. She used *Over-The-Counter Natural Cures Expanded* to help her wean off the meds. Her transformation began. She started applying the three pillars of health—detox, nutrient logic, and hormone intelligence—to initiate her path toward living young. Like resurrecting a dying plant, her body began to heal itself. She also boosted her stamina!

Within two months, Katrina was off insulin! With no more diabetes, the weight began to melt off thanks to her newly optimized hormone balance, output, and sensitivity.

Katrina was fighting for her life. Fighting focuses the mind and heightens the senses. Lighter in weight, and with more room to move, Katrina kept smashing. Her body began its natural detox methods to remove metabolic, chemical, and environmental waste. Nutrient logic restored her deficiencies. The three pillars of health were slowly bringing her back from the dead.

"Off my meds, my A1C levels dropped to 6.2. On meds it was over 10. My triglycerides were 800, now 101! Numbers don't lie, like you say, it's all about measurable results."

"I was off all my meds in only 7 months. I lost 100 pounds!"

"Shane, you gave me the information, tools, and products I needed to change my life forever. I had my 1 yr anniversary last Thursday and weighed in at 139.8 lbs! Total of 136.2 lbs lost—down to size 6 pants and size medium shirt."

"I actually jump out of bed in the morning! I spend the weekends playing with my daughter. We go fishing, play at the park, walk around the neighborhood, ride bikes, play basketball in the driveway. Everything parents should be doing with their kids."

"My friends and family say they've never personally met anyone who has lost over 100 lbs before without having gastric bypass surgery."

"Oh, and I've never been able to shop for regular misses clothing. I've always been a plus size girl, even in middle and high school. Lane Bryant was my shop of choice. I went in there a couple months ago to get a new pair of work pants and their smallest size fell off of me. I literally didn't know where to go to shop for clothes! I had to ask some girlfriends where to get some regular size clothes! It's a whole new world."

Katrina's success story shows what's possible when you ditch the meds and save yourself from doctor's orders. There's still hope for those who've been afflicted with OBOI. You must start by looking around and making the simple observation that meds are the problem, not the solution.

No drug can do what Katrina did for herself: fight back against a criminal status quo that's been bullying and beating down patients for decades in the name of health care.

Now it's your turn. Ditch the meds, fight back, and live young using my three pillars of health:

1. Detox
2. Nutrient logic
3. Hormone intelligence

When you begin putting these 3 pillars of health to work, your body becomes its own best healer. Sensational health and happiness rebounds and you get a new lease on life. Take your first step by visiting www.DitchTheMeds.com and sign up for my free 30-day start guide.

Once you sign-up at www.DitchTheMeds.com, I'll send you the exact same plan my family and I follow. You'll also receive a free 18-

Minute Workout App, updates on what the latest medical research reveals and even huge discounts on select products mentioned in *3 Worst Meds!* Think of it as your sure-fire shield from confirmation bias as well as pharmaceutical conditioning and corruption. But most importantly, it's your first step to ditching the meds to live a healthier more active life with the 3 pillars of health!

APPENDIX

Free Laboratory Assays

As part of my Blue Diamond Series, I've tested all of the recommended products in this book and included the QC test results free of charge in the figures that follow.

You can't choose supplements based on how pretty a label is, how many celebrities promote it, or because you saw it on Dr. Oz. Currently, there's no governing body to dictate how a botanical medicine should be tested for Quality Control (QC). Therefore, you have no idea what you're getting, ever! The only way to choose a true botanical product is to verify its purity and potency using state-of-the-art chemistry testing methods.

I use techniques known as High-Performance-Liquid-Chromatography (HPLC) and sometimes Nuclear Magnetic Resonance (NMR). These are the same QC methods I used as a medicinal chemist for Big Pharma and my own company, The People's Chemist.

My QC methodology validates that all suggested products are naturally sourced (botanical) and not made in a lab (synthetic). I also carefully screen for impurities such as pesticides, heavy metals, preservatives, and microbes from viral or bacterial contamination.

And most importantly, I measure the active, medicinal ingredients in every batch. In other words, if it was an orange extract being sold as a natural source of vitamin C, my testing would differentiate between ascorbic acid—often sold as "vitamin-C"—and naturally occurring vitamin C. It also verifies the quantity. Nobody else provides that deep level of quality verification. In total, my QC tests guarantee that every product is natural, non-toxic and safe to ingest.

As part of my *Blue Diamond Series*, I've tested all of the recommended products in this book and included the QC test results free of charge in the figures below. A matter of life and death, this razor-sharp laboratory precision is glossed over or even left out by doctors and online vitamin hucksters!

Below, I've included a sample QC chart for Centrum Multivitamin to "warm you up" for viewing the QC charts for each product mentioned in *3 Worst Meds*. You'll notice that it fails my QC standards, miserably.

My QC test shows that Centrum Mulit-Vitamin for adults is loaded with synthetic ingredients and doesn't deliver a single nutrient from nature, as verified by natural HPLC standards. And while it is still technically "United States Pharmacopeia (USP) grade" and free of contamination, it's still unhealthy. This single test proves how today's so-called quality standards are delivering false, synthetic products to unassuming consumers. In comparison, the QC tests for all the suggested products prove their natural origins and purity, thus ensuring safety and efficacy.

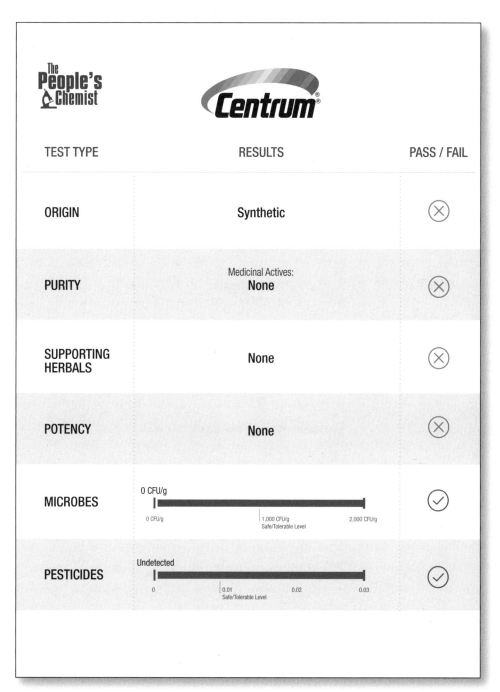

FIGURE 1. The People's Chemist QC Analysis for Centrum Multi-Vitamin.

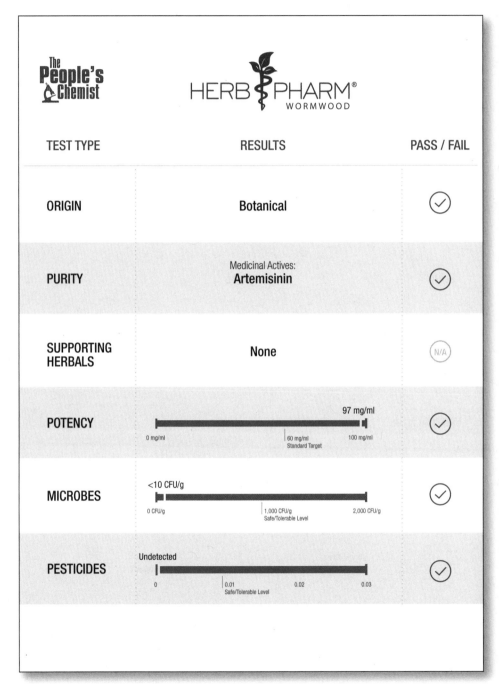

FIGURE 2. The People's Chemist QC Analysis for Herb Pharm Wormwood.

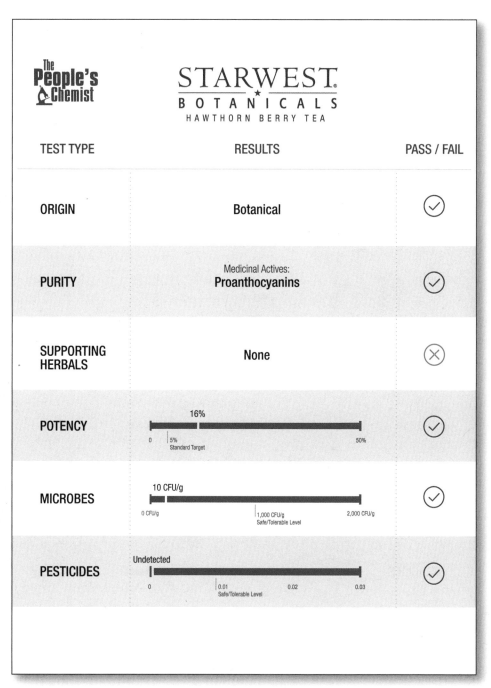

FIGURE 3. The People's Chemist QC Analysis for Starwest Botanical Hawthorn Berry Tea.

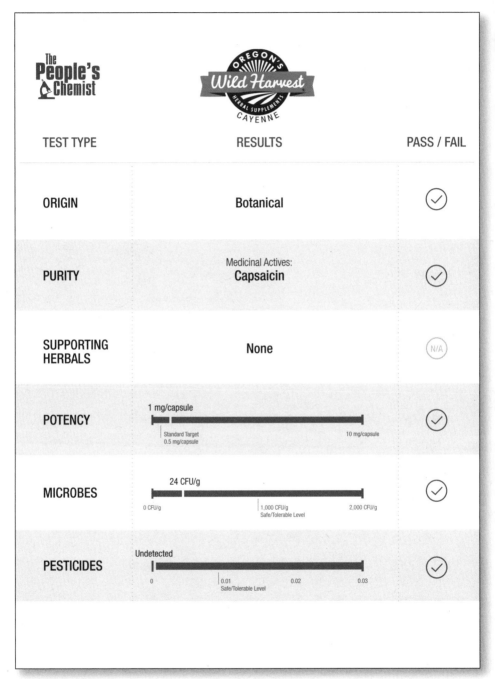

FIGURE 4. The People's Chemist QC Analysis for Wild Harvest Cayenne.

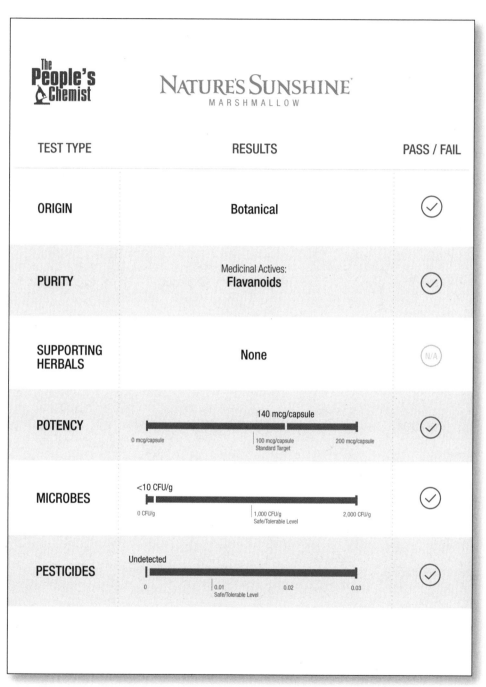

FIGURE 5. The People's Chemist QC Analysis for Nature's Sunshine Marshmallow.

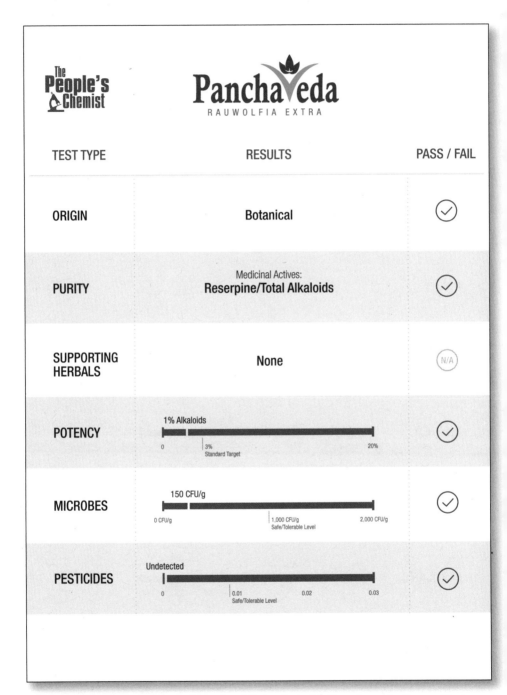

FIGURE 6. The People's Chemist QC Analysis for Panchaveda Rauwolfia Extra Capsules.

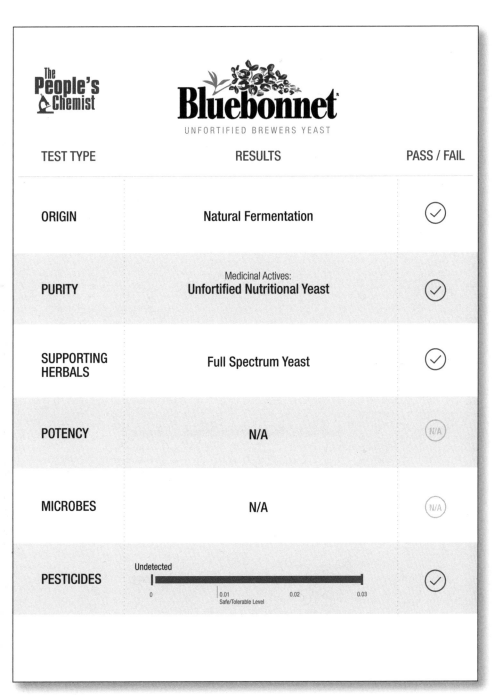

FIGURE 7. The People's Chemist QC Analysis for BlueBonnet Unfortified Brewers Yeast.

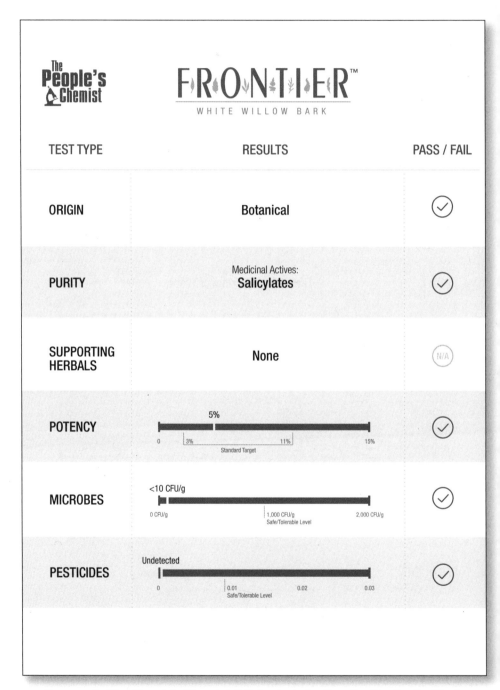

FIGURE 8. The People's Chemist QC Analysis for Frontier Co-Op Certified Organic White Willow Bark Tea.

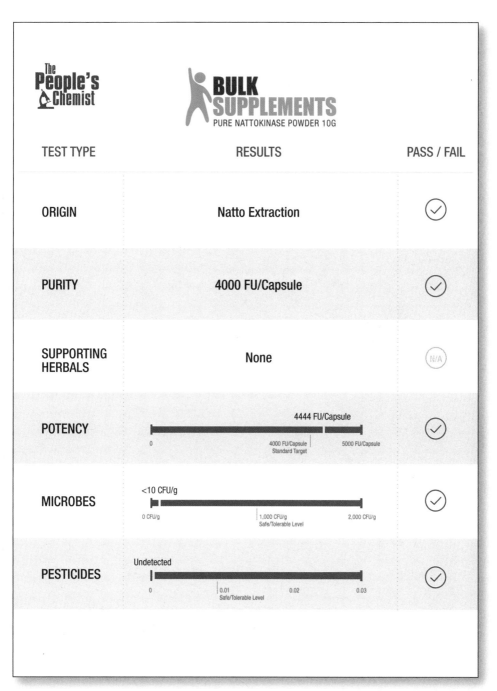

FIGURE 9. The People's Chemist QC Analysis for Bulk Supplements Pure Nattokinase Powder 10g.

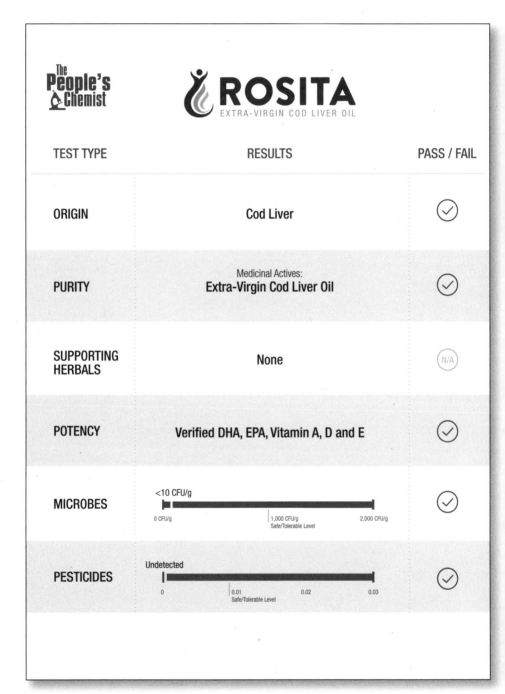

FIGURE 10. The People's Chemist QC Analysis for Rosita Real Foods Extra-Virgin Cod Liver Oil.